THE HAUNTED SOUTH

Two Volumes in One

by

Nancy Roberts

BARNES
&NOBLE
B O O K S
NEW YORK

Originally published in two volumes: *The Haunted South* and
Ghosts of the Southern Mountains and Appalachia

VOLUME ONE:
The Haunted South

Originally published in 1970 as *This Haunted Southland*
Also published as *This Haunted Southland Where Ghosts Still Roam*

Copyright © 1988 by the University of South Carolina

VOLUME TWO:
Ghosts of the Southern Mountains and Appalachia

Copyright © 1978 by Bruce and Nancy Roberts
Copyright © 1988 by the University of South Carolina

This edition published by Barnes & Noble, Inc.,
by arrangement with the University of South Carolina Press

1996 Barnes & Noble Books

ISBN 0-76070-367-1

Printed and bound in the United States of America

96 97 98 99 00 M 9 8 7 6 5 4 3 2 1

FG

Volume One

THE HAUNTED SOUTH

Contents

Prologue

We believe there are spirits who walk this land and we would like to introduce some of them to you as you read this book.

They are the spirits of the people, both good and bad, who forded the rivers, climbed the hills and cultivated the fields which are our inheritance—men and women who loved and fought and gave the land we call "home" names like Gold Hill, Kings Mountain and Wizard Clip.

Housing developments now cover the countryside where hundreds of miners, many from foreign lands, once worked in the Carolina gold fields. Modern highways slash through hills where King George's men stood in resplendent battle lines. But the builders and developers have only destroyed the physical appearance of the area. They can never kill the ghosts and spirits which must rise at night as surely as does the full moon.

And the supernatural is far from remote. It is a matter of daily experience for those who look for more than mediums and witchcraft can never offer.

C. S. Lewis once said, "There is no neutral ground in the universe. Every square inch, every split second, is claimed by God and counterclaimed by Satan." The spirits in this book have fought for both sides and there are others who don't appear to have been on any particular side, but dazed by death and perchance in some sort of limbo, they still return to the land they knew in life.

The ghosts in these pages have an attachment for certain places and when you read these stories, we hope you will understand why. For they do not respect the deed books at the county court house. This is THEIR land and they plan to be here through countless centuries, if they so choose. For a time we feared that progress would eliminate spirits but now that we know them better, we become more convinced that the spirits will not only endure, but will outlast "progress."

Bruce and Nancy Roberts
February 4, 1971

P.S. For those who don't believe in ghosts we have a remedy. The first night of the full moon in October walk to the top of Kings Mountain and then down the path to Colonel Ferguson's grave. Spend the next night watching the Brown Mountain lights alone from a deserted overlook on the Blue Ridge Parkway. And, on the third night go alone at midnight to the Devil's Tramping Ground near Siler City and wait for the moon to set. This will help restore your faith.

THE HAUNTED SOUTH

Passenger Train Number 9

She was sure she had seen a horrible train wreck, but the stationmaster said there had not been a wreck

Do people have premonitions of fearful events which are going to happen to them in the future? How can we tell how often premonitions like this come true, especially if the people are no longer here to tell us.

The baggage master was a tall thin man with a prominent nose and fair skin so transparent the bony structure of his face could be plainly seen beneath it. His eyebrows were a sandy color tipped with gray and the blue eyes which peered out from beneath them had a surprising degree of sparkle and humor. Right now he was scrutinizing his watch observing that it was almost one o'clock in the morning and satisfied that all the baggage was loaded and the train would be leaving Salisbury for Asheville, North Carolina, in a few minutes.

The steam engine spewed forth smoke and cinders, the cry of the whistle was a thin, earsplitting shriek in the stillness of the early morning. The baggage master's name was H. K. Linster and he was from Statesville where he usually got off for a few minutes to chat with friends. He frowned as he snapped the case of his large lavishly engraved gold watch shut and prepared to board the train. Was there a hint of reluctance in his step? Did he feel any differently tonight than on the hundreds of nights before?

But that was many years ago, early morning of August 27th, 1891 to be exact, and our story has more to do with the summer vacation trip of a family from Columbia, S.C.

There was nothing unusual about the way it all started. Pat and Larry Hayes had been planning their mountain vacation for a long time. Not that they could really afford a trip what with Larry having only been in business for himself a year, but they both knew the whole family needed it.

The borrowed camper would save money and although Pat knew little about camping, she was game to learn and the children were old enough to help. Larry was not through work until late and it was after ten when Pat put the extra bedding in the trunk and they were ready to go. Larry decided he would let Pat drive from Columbia, South Carolina, to Charlotte, North Carolina, and he would drive the next lap to Statesville which was not far from Pat's mother's home.

At the filling station where they stopped in Charlotte, the station attendant commented that one of the tires was low and Larry agreed that he should fill it with more air. By now the children were asleep and Pat laid her silver blonde head back on a pillow wedged between the seat and the door so that she could nap.

Larry drove silently, following the road almost automatically, while his thoughts were on the past year and his efforts to build up his business. Sud-

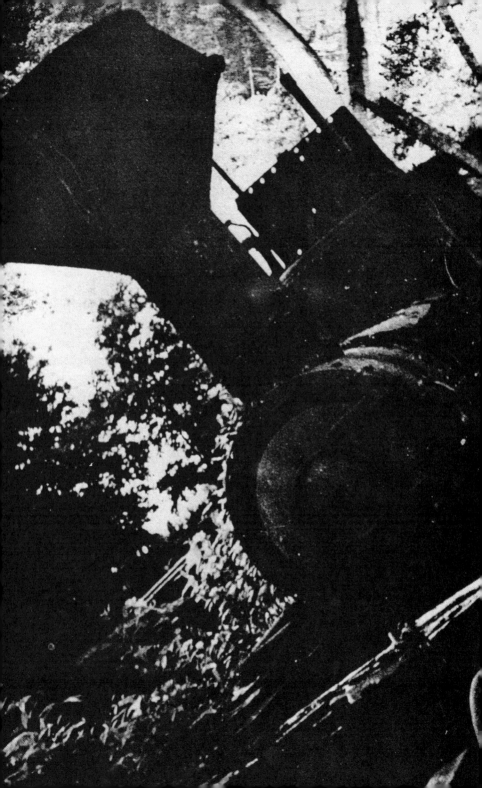

denly, he felt the wheel twist beneath his hand and the car begin to go toward the other side of the road. He realized the tire had blown and the weight of the trailer was making it more difficult for him to control the car. Pat was immediately awake but she did not scream or cry out. Luckily he managed to slow the car, guide it back into his own lane and off the road onto the safety of the shoulder.

Larry got out to look for the jack so that he could change the tire. He and Pat both searched the back of the car but no jack. Then Pat remembered. She had left the jack on the floor of the garage when she rearranged the camping supplies.

It was almost three o'clock in the morning, there were no cars along the road at this hour and Larry figured the best thing to do was to go for help. He remembered a country store he had noticed just before the blowout. There was a light on in the back and he suspected the store owner might live there.

The children complained drowsily, then one by one fell asleep again. Pat sat wide awake and somewhat nervous but reassured by Larry's certainty that it was only a short distance back to the store.

She heard the whistle of a train far off in the distance and as it came closer she thought of how mournful a train whistle late at night can sound. Then a light appeared, at first no bigger than a pinpoint, and she watched it advance closer and closer until it was just a few hundred yards from the car.

It was the headlight on the engine and she could now see the engine and the coaches quite clearly. The train had begun to cross the bridge and had just reached the center when she was aghast to see the engine, cab and coaches give a convulsive lurch, leave the track and hurtle through the air, plunging off the bridge down into the darkness and out of sight. There were crashing, wrenching sounds as metal and wood tore asunder and cars smashed against each other.

This was followed by the most frightful screams, men's and women's voices intermingled, pleading for help. Horror-stricken, Pat jumped out of the car and began running in the direction from which the screams came. When she reached the bank of the stream and looked down below her, it was a sickening sight. The engine, tender, coaches and pullman cars were a huge pile of debris jutting out in every direction and completely damming up the creek.

People were climbing through broken windows, some being pulled through by those who had crawled out first and there were yet others who had fallen into the stream and were trying to swim to the bank. Adding to the danger and perilous situation of survivors was the fact that, dammed up by the wreckage, the water in the stream was rising and entering the railroad cars.

In the midst of all the cries and groans Pat became aware that there was a man standing next to her. He was dressed in what must have been a railroad uniform and beneath the visor of his hat she could see that his face looked extremely white. No wonder, after what this poor man had just gone through.

"Can you give me the time, Ma'am? I would like to check my watch and see if it is running properly," said the trainman. He was gazing down at a large gold watch which she noticed with surprise looked just like the old-fashioned watch her grandfather used to show her when she was a child. But no doubt, railroad men still carried watches like this.

"It is five minutes past three," she replied. "I wish I could go for help, but we just had a blowout and I will have to wait until my husband comes back." The man looked at her strangely and did not answer. She began to feel very much afraid. Then his face started to blur and she thought, I must be going to faint, that is why his face seems to be fading away like this.

At that moment she heard the slam of a car door and voices behind her. There was Larry and someone was with him. She ran toward them.

"Larry, there's been a terrible train wreck!" she cried out. Larry and the stranger held a flashlight before them and the three made their way as quickly as possible in the direction she led them over at the side of the bridge. They looked down.

"Where? What in the world are you talking about? There's no train wreck down there," said Larry, the beam of his flashlight probing the stream and the banks.

"For heaven's sake, honey, you've just had some kind of nightmare. This is Mr. Bradley. He's come to help me fix the tire. Come on now, let's go back to the car. You probably fell asleep and when you woke up your dream was real to you."

Dazed, Pat got into the car, and checked the children. They were still asleep, completely unaware that anything unusual had happened.

On the way to her mother's home, Pat told Larry about seeing the train approach, the horrifying wreck and the trainman who had come up to the car. He promised to go by the railroad station the next morning and, if she wished, even back to where she was so certain she had seen the wreck. Larry was still convinced, however, that she had fallen asleep and dreamed about the wreck and the trainman who had asked her what time it was.

The next day they went by the railroad station. The old man at the counter listened while Pat told him about the train going off the track.

"No, there was no wreck last night. There hasn't been a wreck in years on that stretch of track."

"At least not since the wreck of 1891," he said. "My father used to talk about that wreck. It was the most terrible train wreck that ever happened in this state. The train had left Salisbury for Asheville and it got to Bostian's Bridge about three o'clock in the morning. It must have been a dreadful sight to see. They say the train engine and coaches just plunged right off the track and down ninety feet into the stream below the trestle. My father got out there pretty soon and he saw people climbing out the windows and calling for help. But what made it even worse was the coaches dammed up the stream and lots of those people drowned."

"It happened . . . let's see. That's odd. Looks like it was about fifty year ago. I think there's a clipping from an old paper called The Charlotte *Chronicle* in a scrapbook in my drawer."

He rummaged in the drawer, producing a scrapbook full of clippings about promotions, retirement pictures, buildings renovations and other miscellaneous news affecting the railroad over a period of many years. Finally, he came to a yellowed clipping from The Charlotte *Chronicle* of August 28, 1891. It was headlined, "Hurled to Death, Thirty Killed, Many Injured. At Three O'clock in the Morning, Bridge Near Statesville The Scene of the Wreck."

"You know the baggage master, a man named H. K. Linster from right here in Statesville, was killed in the wreck. He usually got off and chatted with my dad for a few minutes. What a terrible thing that must have been. I sure would hate to have seen it."

Pat Hayes' face turned white and her head began to swim. It seemed that the inside of the railroad station was beginning to go around and around. She held on to the edge of the counter and closed her eyes for a minute. But that was worse! For then she could see the light of a train followed by the engine and the coaches as they twisted and lurched before they hurtled off the track and down into the darkness. The lights in the coaches streaked through her mind like fireworks going off and again and again she could hear the screams.

18

"Lady, lady, are you all right?" The station master was holding her elbow.

"I didn't mean to upset you none. After all, that wreck happened fifty years ago. In fact, it was exactly fifty years ago last night."

The Little People

"I saw them with my own eyes. They were on the mountain, they were near the rock . . . they were everywhere!"

There are still some wild and unexplored places left in the mountains of Western North Carolina and one about which many weird tales continue to be told is Hickory Nut Gorge near Chimney Rock.

The gorge is a challenge to even the most bold and experienced. There are precipitate cliffs, narrow ledges to scale and dizzying heights, and the reward may be bottomless pools, spectacular waterfalls seen by few and grotesque rock formations.

Nor far from this gorge on the thirty-first of July 1806, a Presbyterian minister and teacher at Newton Academy sat at his desk preparing his lesson for the following day's classes. He was so absorbed in his work that it was almost eight o'clock when he realized the light had gone and the pleasant breeze which had stirred the curtains at the window next to his desk now had an icy bite.

He closed the window, found the white china matchbox, lit the kerosene lamps and touched a match to the fire. As the flames blazed up he heard

Chimney Rock where the Little People were seen on several occasions

footsteps on the porch and an agitated pounding at his door.

Hurrying through the dark hall he bumped into the sharp, curving arms of the coat rack on his way to the front door. When he opened it there stood his friend, Robert Searcy.

"I don't know how to tell you what I have just seen" said Searcy. "You may not even believe me, but I saw them with my own eyes. They were on the mountain, they were near the rock, they were everywhere! May I come in and sit down?" His face was white and he appeared genuinely shaken.

"Of course, you may. But who in the world are you talking about and what have you seen?"

"Well, no matter how I tell you about this it is going to sound like I have lost my mind, but probably the best thing for me to do is start at the beginning. As I sat on my porch reading after an early supper, Mrs. Reaves' girl came running up to tell me there was a crowd of people flying around on the side of the mountain near the Rock and to come right away. I simply dismissed what she said as probably some children playing a prank.

"But a few minutes later Mrs. Reaves herself came and begged me to go with her to see the 'ghosties' as she called them. This poor superstitious woman is really upset, I told myself, and deciding that the kindest thing I could do was to go with her to calm her, we started toward the mountain. After a few minutes she said, 'Do you see them?'

"I saw nothing at all and told her so. We walked a little further and she grasped my arm saying, 'There they are. Look! Over there.' This time as I looked toward the Chimney, I was absolutely amazed for south of Chimney Rock and floating along the side of the mountain was a huge crowd of white, phantom-like beings. Their clothing, and filmy as it looked, I can only call it 'clothing,' was so brilliant a white it almost hurt my eyes to look at them. But they appeared to be human, for I could see that there were men and women and children, all sizes of beings, even infants.

"As I watched, two of them who appeared to be men went on ahead of the crowd, coming quite close to the Rock, and then vanished."

"What a frightening experience," said Newton.

"No, that is the oddest part of it," replied Searcy. "Although I felt weak, somehow, it left a solemn and

pleasing impression on my mind. But you must think I have surely gone crazy. Tell me, is that what has happened? Is this the beginning of some strange insanity?"

Robert Searcy searched his friend's face anxiously for an answer. Smoke curled upward from Newton's pipe. He frowned thoughtfully and looked toward the window with its drawn curtains as if he were trying to see through them and out to the gorge for a glimpse of the mysterious beings Searcy had described.

"Don't just sit there! Tell me, friend. Am I going insane?" shouted Searcy.

"No, no. Now calm down," Newton raised one hand palm outward toward his friend. "You are not going crazy at all. You have simply seen a sight that only a few people have ever been privileged to witness. A sight so spectacular that stories about it have been told for generations among the Cherokee Indians. You recall that this whole area was once the country of the Cherokee Nation."

"For heavens sake, George, do I need a history lesson at a time like this? What does that have to do with the white figures I saw floating along the mountainside?"

"I am telling you this because the Cherokees knew about them."

"Knew about who?"

"The Little People. Do you think that something like you saw this afternoon has never happened before? Of course it has. Rare, yes, and it may have been years ago and it may not happen for many years hence."

"The gorge was the gateway to the country where the tobacco the Indians wanted for their pipes grew. It was always a frightening place to the Indians, but it was not so much the difficulties of travelling through it, the bottomless pools, the eerie rock formations which appear to us like frightful giants of another age. Nor was it the savage force with which the wind sweeps through that gorge, tearing away plants and leaving the rock bare. Oh, no. It was not these things that kept them from travelling through the gorge to reach the land where the tobacco grew. It was the spirits, the little people themselves or whatever you wish to call them, that guarded the gateway through the mountains."

"Tonight you have seen what no man may see again for years. I don't know how to explain them. You say that you saw men, women and children. If they were a mirage it is strange that a mirage would have stayed in the area long enough for Mrs. Reaves to have sent her daughter, then come after you herself. Also, a mirage is more often seen by one person,

perhaps due to their physical or mental state at the moment, rather than by several."

"Could these 'beings' be angels?" asked Searcy.

"Angels? I really don't know. I have never been a great believer in spirits from another world making themselves visible in our own, but if I had been fortunate enough to see that fantastic crowd of white robed figures floating across the mountainside as you did this afternoon, I might change my mind!

"You must see it, too. It was tremendous! When do you think it might happen again?"

"My dear Robert, how am I possibly to guess when it will happen again. We have no idea what causes them to appear. But, I would say that it is possible for the same condition present this evening to occur at another time and when they do, whoever is near the Rock will see the figures just as you did."

Mr. Newton's prediction has come true on more than one occasion since.

In 1811 a similar phenomenon was seen. So large was the crowd that some compared it to a battle with "swords flashing" but this was probably inaccurately described. Again, shortly after the Civil War the entire countryside talked of seeing The Little People.

But the phenomenon is reported only rarely and probably when someone does see it, they are reluctant to talk of the experience, especially in these days of technology and the computer.

Some scoffers have suggested that all that was ever seen in the gorge were cloud formations, although we wonder whether intelligent observers can mistake clouds for "men, women and children."

The Phantom Rider
of the Confederacy

*The General reached for his pistol and aimed it
at the oncoming rider when to his astonishment
he saw the scores of bullet holes in the cape which
floated in the wind*

It is really a shame that Ichabod Crane and the
Headless Horseman on the Tarrytown Road in New
York ever managed to get so much publicity for the
headless horseman. For the horseman there was a
trickster who carried a pumpkin under his arm and
not a head.

For years while people have been reading about
this nonsense up at Tarrytown, they have ignored the
real Phantom Rider of the Confederacy who rides a
palomino stallion. She wears gossamer garments
which float behind her and her blond hair streams in
the wind. Both hands grasp the reins as she comes
out of the past, is visible only briefly, and vanishes
into the darkness as if all the legions of another world
were in pursuit.

The main highway South through Arden and
Fletcher past the old Calvary Episcopal Church has

long since been paved. But this has not stopped the pounding of the palomino's hoofbeat which can be heard on the shoulder of the road.

Reverend Charles Stewart McClellan, Jr., writing in the Southern Tourist Magazine in December 1926, was the first writer to compare the Phantom Rider of the South with the Legend of Sleepy Hollow.

"There is a horseman who often rides through the night around old Calvary Church at Fletcher."

He tells the story of a very beautiful girl who lived near the church and was in love with a Confederate soldier whom her family refused to let her marry. Eventually, her suitor was ordered away to join Braxton Bragg's army at Chattanooga and her parents still held steadfast to their decision that she would never marry a Confederate.

During the days of the war the well at Calvary Church where she met her suitor was called "the wishing well" and local legends said that if you wished hard enough before you drank from the well your wish would come true. Even after he had gone she often went to their meeting place. But the day came when she received word that her beloved had been killed.

So, the story goes that our maiden did not wish to live but only to join the one she loved. Her father paid little heed when she told him her wish would come true and so it did, just as if she had willed her own death.

The evening after the funeral service the Jenkinses sat in silence on the porch of their farm home near Fletcher Road. It was early autumn and the leaves of the dogwood trees, already turned a brilliant red, fluttered in the wind. It appeared as if the air, which was especially cold, came from among the pine trees

in the church yard and the graveyard with its freshly covered grave.

The wind blew in such gusts that a faint chiming sound seemed to come from the church bells. And then in the distance came the pound of hoofbeats. On and on they came. Past the church, past the graveyard, riding with a strange, inexorable quality straight toward the Jenkins home.

Jenkins had never seen such an awesome sight. The hoofs scarcely seemed to touch the ground. But what terrified him was the palomino horse. For it was the horse of Lieutenant C. A. Walpole and on the horse was a young woman wearing a Confederate cavalry cape to protect her against the cold. He recognized now both the horse and rider. The girl was his daughter buried only the day before and the horse had been sent by the spirit of the young lieutenant to bring her.

Her last wish by the old well had come true.

Directly in front of Jenkins, the horse and its rider stopped. But while the horse stood motionless the wind and dust swirled up in a cloud and from it a voice spoke.

"Father, you have doomed me to ride forever. Do you known how bitter cold the wind is?" and leaves swept fiercely about the horse's hooves.

"Next spring General Stoneman and his troops will be here. They will burn your farm thinking you are a Confederate sympathizer because I will lead them here and they will chase this horse to your barn."

And it came about just as the girl had said. For in the spring of 1865 General Stoneman and his men rode into Fletcher just as dusk was falling across the graveyard and the shadows of the tall pines lay upon the tombstones.

The General was in an angry mood. His advance scouting party had been ambushed on the outskirts of Asheville and the major, who had barely escaped with his life, was describing how he and his men had been lured into the trap chasing a Confederate courier on a palomino horse.

"And the strangest thing happened. Just as the horse was about to pull away from us it turned and started to charge back. I ordered my men to stop and every trooper fired at the rider. The horse reared up as if to laugh at us and then from both sides of the road we were ambushed. Twenty-three of my men were killed. I chased after the rider and I fired my pistol six times. I have never missed my mark before and those bullets went right through him."

General Stoneman was obviously upset and irritated.

"Major, you must be extremely overtired and overwrought. I will dispatch Captain Butler to track down the rider."

A short time later the Captain picked up the trail of a single horse and followed it to a farm not far from Calvary Church. The farm belonged to a man named Jenkins who had died that winter. Butler searched the area but could not find the lone rider. However, he believed that the farm was being used as a refuge by the Confederates so he set fire to not only the house but the buildings around it.

From his headquarters camped at Calvary Church, General Stoneman wandered over to the well. It was past midnight, but the general still could not sleep. It was very seldom any of his men were ambushed and he was puzzled by the conduct of his commanding officer who was noted for his excellent marksmanship.

"I wish I could see that rider myself," he mused as he reached down and picked up the dipper at the well. The instant the water touched his lips he saw flames rising from the Jenkins farmhouse and congratulated himself on a problem solved.

As he turned to walk back across the church yard to his headquarters tent, a dark rider galloped across the field. For a moment he thought it was Butler so he did not call out to the sentries. But the rider did not slow, and then, in a split second, he realized the figure mounted upon the horse was not a Union soldier.

He reached for his pistol and aimed it at the horseman's head when to his astonishment he saw

31

The iron gates at the end of the church drive never barred the Phantom Rider

that the rider was a woman and there were scores of bullet holes in the cape which floated in the wind behind her. He lowered his gun and watched as horse and rider rushed past him and disappeared down the road. So quickly had the horse come and gone that even the startled sentries had not been able to fire.

There were many things the general knew about war and he was not about to lose another man chasing a ghost. Not a single rider did General Stoneman dispatch to give chase. He looked at the red glow of the flames in the sky and as the road turned and rose at the crest of the hill for a brief second the ghostly rider was silhouetted in the crimson of the horizon. Strangely enough this was the only building ever burned in the Fletcher area.

A few weeks later the war came to a close and the stories of the phantom rider were classified with this period when emotions ran high and violence filled the air.

But, according to Reverend McClellan some years later, two young men of Fletcher were riding along the ridge road one night and one, as he was adjusting his stirrup strap, heard the approach of another horse. As he stood next to his own mount he could clearly see the phantom rider who dashed up to him, gazed curiously at him for a moment, and then galloped away into the night. He also tells of a farmer returning to the Fletcher settlement very late one night who was drowsy and fell asleep on his horse. The horse knew the road and kept on but suddenly the farmer was awakened by the clatter of a horse's hooves.

When he awoke and saw the Rider he sank into unconsciousness and the next day when he came to in his barn, he told his friends the story of his midnight encounter with the Phantom Rider.

And so, there will probably always be accounts of hoofbeats in the night and a mysterious figure on horseback amidst the wooded quiet of Calvary Church, and the old graveyard will continue to provide a refuge for the ghosts of those who frequented this area during its violent and colorful past. A past when the Phantom Rider of the Confederacy, with her cape blown by the wind, sped through the night down the old Fletcher Road, her steed's hoofbeats in the distance coming closer and closer, past the church, past the graveyard, riding on and on and on.

The old Church is still there, the graveyard, the road—and when the night is dark and windy, who knows who else?

The Demon of Wizard Clip

All around them people could hear the
clip-clip of the demoniacal shears

The devil ensnares the sons of men in strange and devious ways. And down to this very day the memory of the evil wrought by one of his minions still hangs like a dank fog over an ancient village in West Virginia.

The village bears three names, Smithfield, Middle-

way and oddest of all—Wizard Clip.

Through it ran the principal wagon route from Baltimore to Southwest Virginia, Kentucky and Tennessee. But the wagoneers have long been dead. With them died the fortunes of Wizard Clip and the man who helped it get its name.

Our story starts near the beginning of the nineteenth century with a Pennsylvanian named Livingstone. Leaving his native state he and his family purchased a lakeside farm on the outskirts of the town we have mentioned. In front of his farm and beside the Opequon River ran the wagon road.

A man of mild temperament, the Pennsylvanian was fond of contrasting with a certain modest air his former failures and the success he was enjoying in his new home.

Although Livingstone himself was liked well enough by his neighbors, the same could not be said of his wife. She was a woman of mean and dominating disposition who kept much to herself.

The Livingstones had lived only a few years in their new home when the event which was to cause their undoing befell them. Appropriately enough it happened on a most miserably cold and rainy night. Gusts of wind screeched plaintively outside the Livingstone's windows and tore with icy fingers at the shutters.

They had readied themselves for bed and were about to ensconce themselves under their feather comforters when Mrs. Livingstone heard a faint sound on the porch, quickly followed by a loud knock.

Her husband went to the door, cautiously cracking it open a few inches, only to have the force of the wind wrest it from his hand. In front of him stood the tall figure of a man, cloak swirling madly about him in the gale.

"I pray you will give me a night's lodging, sir," begged Livingstone's visitor. "My wagon has suffered an accident to a wheel and cannot be repaired before morning."

"We are about to retire but will be glad to have you pass the night with us," replied Livingstone although he could see the dour look on the face of his wife.

The stranger came in and without much grace Mrs. Livingstone showed him to his room.

The house had not been settled and quiet for long when in addition to the eerie wail of the wind another sound could be heard. It was a succession of fearsome groans interspersed with the sharp outcries of a man in pain. Stopping only to jerk on his slippers, Livingstone hurried to the door of the stranger's room and asked him if all was well with him.

In a tortured voice his guest replied that he was deathly ill and did not expect to live to see daylight. He begged his host to summon a Catholic priest that he might be given the last rites, admitting the he had neglected his religion in health, but now, in extremis, felt in dire need of its consolation.

Livingstone replied that he knew of no priest nearby and couldn't hope to find one closer than Maryland. He remarked, however, that his neighbors—the McSherrys and the Minghinis—were Catholic and perhaps could tell him of one.

His wife was by now listening to the conversation and at this she became extremely angry.

"If you think you are going to start out on any such wild goose chase in the middle of the night, I shall take good care to thwart you," said she. "And even if you should succeed in finding one, I warn you, no Romish priest shall ever set foot in my house!"

The turnpike in front of the Livingstone house looked much like this road near Wizard Clip

"The best thing you can do is return to your bed. I'll wager this guest of ours will be as well as you or I by morning. And if I have my way he shall be on his way with the sun's first rays."

Livingstone reluctantly gave in to his wife and went back to bed.

All night the pitiful pleas and outcries continued. Next morning their guest did not appear and, much alarmed, Livingstone entered his room.

The stranger was dead.

Of course, a story had to be decided upon to tell the neighbors. The Livingstones simply said that a wayfarer had asked lodging with them the night before and died in his sleep. They made no mention of his dying wish. They recalled with surprise that he had not told them his name and, search his belongings as they would, no clue could be found to his identity.

A simple funeral was held late the following evening and the unknown traveler laid to rest. The family had no sooner returned home and were gathered around the fire discussing the day's events when the logs in the fireplace began to writhe and jump as if in agony.

Soon they were whirling all about the room in a horrible sort of dance. After them danced Livingstone trying to catch them and heave them back into the fireplace. But no sooner would he return them than what seemed to be an almost demoniacal power would toss them out again.

This went on all night long and the terrified family did not get a moment's rest.

The following morning the worn out Livingstone went down to the highway in front of his house. He had just reached the road when he was accosted by an irate wagoneer who had stopped his team there. "What the devil do you mean barring a public road with a rope?" cried the fellow. "Untie it from those trees, you rascal."

Livingstone rubbed his tired eyes in bewilderment. He was sure the man was drunk for he could see no rope at all. Becoming more furious by the minute the driver drew a knife and made as if to approach Livingstone. But instead he slashed at the air before him.

Now it was the wagoneer's turn to be amazed. For his knife met no resistance at all. Only airy nothingness. While he stood there in bewilderment debating what to do next another team arrived and its driver went through the same performance with the same outcome.

At length Livingstone mildly suggested that they drive on regardless of the spectre rope, and this they did. But all that day each new arrival brought Livingstone a fresh cursing. And so it kept up for several weeks.

By now it was obvious to the Livingstones and their neighbors that the strange events taking place could only be the work of a demon. And soon the Livingstones began to be harassed in yet another way. A sharp clipping noise as from a pair of invisible shears could be heard throughout and around the house. Worse yet all the family clothes and table linens were cut with crescent-shaped slits.

When visitors arrived to console with the Livingstones they would find even the handkerchiefs folded in their pockets covered with the crescent shaped tears. And all around them they could hear the incessant clip-clip of the demoniacal shears.

On one occasion a lady visitor was complimenting Mrs. Livingstone on the fine flock of ducks waddling through the yard on their way to the Opequon River. "Clip-Clip" went the uncanny, invisible shears and, one after another, each duck's head fell to the ground, cleanly decapitated before the ladies' very eyes.

Stories of the "Wizard Clip" were spreading far and wide. And the young men of the neighborhood, eager to show how fearless they were, talked Livingstone into letting them hold a dance there. Despite the terrors of the place curiosity led many young ladies to attend.

One blustering fellow came all the way from Winchester carrying his rifle. He was determined to show off his bravery to his girl and bragged of what he would do to anything trying to clip him. All went smoothly for awhile when suddenly "clip-clip" went the devilish shears and the Winchester hero felt something flap against the back of his legs.

Much to his humiliation he was forced to retreat backwards through the nearest door while the girls looked coyly in another direction.

By this time poor Livingstone was rapidly losing heart and even his wife's masculine courage was dwindling. One night he had a dream.

He thought he was standing at the foot of a hill on top of which stood a man dressed in flowing black robes. The man appeared to be engaged in some sort of religious ceremony. As he looked at him he became aware of the presence of a disembodied voice near him. The voice whispered that the man on the hill could relieve him of the torture he and his family were undergoing.

Believing the garb to be that of a priest, Livingstone immediately sought aid from the Minghinis and the McSherrys. He found that a certain Father Cahill would shortly be at Shepherdstown, about ten miles away, to hold Catholic services.

His neighbors promised Livingstone an introduction to the priest and on the day specified they accompanied their unhappy neighbor to the church meeting.

Livingstone recognized the priest immediately as the figure in his dream and falling down on his knees begged him for help. As tears streamed down his face he poured out the story of his heartlessness toward the stranger and all that had happened thereafter.

Cahill was a big-fisted Irishman not averse to an encounter even with the devil himself. So he consented to accompany Livingstone and do all he could to relieve him.

When he arrived at the Livingstones' home Father Cahill got down on his knees and, holding a small cross in his hands, prayed fervently. Then he sprinkled holy water on the threshold of the house.

"Now you must take me to the place the stranger

is buried," said the priest. Together they went to what is now the old burying ground of Wizard Clip.

As the priest consecrated the grave there was the sound of a great rushing wind through the trees overhead. His robes billowed out from his body, lending an eerie, winged look to the blackgarbed figure.

And the bottomless waters of the nearby lake seethed turbulently as if embracing its own. Close to the village of Wizard Clip the dark waters still hold their secret. The wizard is gone but somehow one has the feeling he may not be far off. And if walking through the village on a rainy afternoon about dusk doesn't convince you the story is true then go to the county clerk's office in Charles Town, West Virginia.

There in the yellowing deed book is the very paper whereby in gratitude to Father Cahill and his successors Livingstone deeded thirty-four acres of land for the exorcising of the fiend. To this day the land is known as "Priest's Field."

Room for One More

*The coachman called "room for one more,"
and this time the invitation seemed to
be meant for her!*

It seemed impossible to the girl getting off the
plane from New York which had just taxied into the
Atlanta airport that such a thing as New York and a
real southern plantation could actually co-exist in the
1950's.

In the late summer she had met Ruthanne Reeves
on a vacation trip to Greece and the two girls had
returned to New York on the same plane. Ruthanne
went back to her plantation home in Georgia and
Elise Barnhardt to her work with a New York pub-
lishing firm.

Ruthanne and "brother John" as she called him,
greeted Elise gaily and as they walked toward John's
tiny sports car brother and sister kept interrupting
each other with talk of parties and plans for the
weekend. The car sped along one country road after
another, seldom going through anything but villages
with a few houses and a country store or two at the
crossroads.

It was dusk and for a few minutes there was that

intense light in which everything takes on a glow all its own. The fragile, spider-like cleome flowers in front of the dark gray unpainted little shacks were a vibrant pink. The cotton fields could not have looked more green.

There was a dreamlike quality about the drive as they passed one shack after another with their rusty tin roofs, sitting lonely, back from the road in the midst of a few pine trees. Then they turned down a dirt road and drove through swamps which hummed and chirped with dusk's surge of life, past gates protecting private roads, and on and on. Finally, they turned down one of these, passing through an open iron gate. Sweet gum and pine branches flicked the side of the car until the woods abruptly ceased.

Ahead lay a long avenue of moss-draped live oaks and beneath these huge olds trees it was always twilight. Under this leafy, moss-draped ceiling a shadowy stillness had settled in broken only by the occasional, mournful sound of a dove.

The last rays of the sun disappeared as the car pulled up in front of an immense, sprawling southern mansion. Tall columns at the front and wings at each side made it look like some grand and dignified creature crouched nobly on its haunches. Lights were flickering on now in the rooms of the house and as the three young people entered the large center hall Ruthanne's mother, a short, cheerful little woman, plump as a marsh hen, greeted them warmly.

That evening friends arrived from nearby towns and plantations for an extremely gay dinner party and dance on the rear piazza which overlooked the river. Elise was entranced. She watched the shimmering trail of the full moon on the black waters of

the river with a delightful young man who managed to make her feel completely feminine and devastatingly attractive.

The party was over shortly after twelve and the girls were tired, so by one-thirty all was quiet. Elise should have fallen asleep quickly but she did not. Her trip, the events of the evening, and even the quiet, so different from all the noises of a city at night, were enough to make her more wakeful. She tossed restlessly on the high fourposter mahogany bed, heard the grandfather clock in the hall strike two and swung her feet over the side of the bed, deciding to get up and draw back the drapes slightly, hoping for a cool breeze.

At that moment she heard a clatter outside which to her startled ears sounded like the clatter of horses' hooves. Reaching the window she drew the drapes and looked out. She could hardly believe her eyes. Directly beneath her window in the circular drive stood an impressive gold and black stagecoach drawn by four gleaming black stallions. Beside it stood a coachman dressed in black coat and britches. The entire scene was illuminated by the light of the full moon. Holding the door of the coach open with one hand, the coachman gestured toward the house with the other and called out—"Room for one more!"

Amazed, she stared down at his face. The skin was swarthy and the lips full above the jutting chin. A long scar staggered irregularly across the man's left cheek, running from the corner of his eye to his mouth.

Before she could recover from her surprise both coach and coachman seemed to literally dissolve into the darkness and disappear. She did not fall asleep until the day broke, she was so frightened, and the next morning she was quite late in awakening.

Ruthanne teased her about the young man she had danced with so frequently the night before and whether she had not tired herself out. Elise smiled somewhat wanly. She was embarrassed yet she felt that she would be more so, if she tried to tell her friend she had seen an old-fashioned carriage and coachman in front of the house in the middle of the night.

That evening everyone gathered again to swim in the river and cook supper along the shore. They were all warm and friendly but as it grew dark, Elise found herself growing somewhat depressed and uneasy; however, she forced herself to talk and joke and somehow the evening passed. At eleven everyone left and the two girls sat down over a glass of iced tea and cookies to talk. But soon Elise felt so irresistibly sleepy that she could not stay up any longer so she told her friend good night.

She fell asleep almost immediately and when she awoke, although it was only about an hour later, she did not know where she was or why she had waked up. In a moment or two she recognized the tall bedposts in the light from the moon streaming in the window and realized she was not in her New York apartment but in the bedroom of the plantation house. From without there came the rhythmic clatter of horses' hooves. She got up quickly and went over to look out. There below the window was the same scene of the night before, the striking black and gold coach and the figure of the coachman standing beside it, holding the door open with a flourish.

"Room for one more!" she heard him call out and tonight as he did so he looked up toward her window and smiled. But the smile was horrifying and made the scar on his cheek stand out with an almost purplish hue in the moonlight. "Room for one more," came the call again and this time the invitation seemed to be meant for her!

Then the coach vanished as mysteriously as it had the night before. Elise was so terrified she literally began to tremble as she sat on the edge of her bed. She did not know whether to leave her room and awaken Ruthanne or whether she would be able to conquer her fear and wait until morning. She went back to the window and looked out but where the coach had stood there was now nothing at all except a pattern of shadows cast by the moonlight upon the white gravel of the drive. A breeze rustled softly through the magnolia leaves and other than that, most of the small night sounds seemed to have fallen asleep. All was quiet and finally Elise, too slept.

The following morning Elise was so exhausted that it was not hard for her to convince Ruthanne she was not feeling well and would like to return to New York. Ruthanne and John were disappointed but considerate enough to help her in every way. Elise had not been able to get a reservation from New York on the flight she wanted. Now she insisted she would go on standby.

When they arrived at the airport she bought her ticket and was told that even though the plane was full, there was always the chance a passenger might not arrive. No one else had gotten there before her to stand by and she would have the first available seat. They watched the big silver plane taxi up. Passengers got off and other passengers with their reservations got on.

As she walked toward the gate she saw the retreating back of the attendant going to the plane to check with the stewardess on whether it was full. She

49

chatted with John and Ruthanne more cheerfully now that she knew she was away from the plantation and would be back in her own apartment that night. This busy airport seemed far away from the world of the Old South as she waited to see whether she would get a seat. Now the gate attendant was returning from checking to see whether there were any empty seats. She heard him call out.

"There is room for one more."

Elise felt a sense of shock go through her entire being. She moved forward so that she could get a better look at the man's face and as she did so he looked directly at her and repeated, "Room for one more!" His eyes met hers and there was a strange half-smile in them. His skin was swarthy, the lips full and red above a jutting chin. A scar ran across his left cheek. It was the face of the driver of the coach! The coachman who had come for her two nights in succession.

Almost hysterical, she asked her friends to take her back to the waiting room. She knew that she was not going to take that plane no matter how eager she was to get home. There was nothing she could do now but tell Ruthanne and John about her experience of the past two nights and they were astounded for neither of them had ever seen the coach or the mysterious coachman, and the plantation had been their home since childhood. However, they were quite sympathetic and it was decided that Elise should wait for a later plane and meanwhile the three would have dinner.

When it was time for her plane to depart they went back to the same gate. All three were curious to see whether the same attendant would be there. Instead they saw a thin, blonde young man with a lightly tanned complexion and a pleasant smile looking over the group of people huddled near the gate waiting for the plane to fill and hoping for a seat.

"Where is the other fellow who has the scar across his face?" Elise asked the gate attendant.

"What fellow with a scar on his face?

"He was here for a flight to New York which left from this gate at twelve-thirty," Elise replied.

"That's impossible, I remember being on this gate myself because when I went to the plane to check on the number of passengers, I was delayed getting back. I stopped to help the stewardess with a door which was sticking. When I did return and called out that there was room for one more, a man with a briefcase under his arm got on the plane. We don't even have anyone like you describe working for us, miss."

Elise told her baffled friends good-by and got on her plane. The take-off was a beautiful one and the trip back to New York uneventful. that night she was too exhausted even to wonder about the strange events of the weekend. She decided she would think about them later and went on to sleep. The next morning she opened the door of her apartment to bring in her milk and morning newspaper. Glancing at the paper she saw the headline "Plane Crashes on Way to New York."

She read the story. The plane had left the same airport she had early yesterday afternoon. It was the flight which had "Room for one more!"

Tavern of Terror

It was a stop on the drover's trail along the winding French Broad River . . . but for some it was the last

There is a stretch of river on the French Broad from Painted Rock near Hot Springs to a place near Marshall, North Carolina that is one of the most beautiful, scenic and wild valleys of eastern America.

It is also a haunted land, eerie even while the sun casts shadows upon the high cliffs and reflects dancing lights upon the river's waters. Standing down by the river's edge one can hear the echoes from the past, for it was here that the drover's trail ran south from Tennessee following the winding course of the French Broad. Herds of cattle, flocks of geese and turkeys passed through this gorge on their way to market in South Carolina.

And every half dozen miles or so along this stretch of river, there was once a tavern or inn where the weary traveler could rest. Almost all of these tavern people were honest men, good hosts, caring for men and cattle alike. But there was one tavern along the

52

Clarkson laid his gold watch and chain on the bench beside the lantern

river that was not like the rest.

And should you walk today along the banks of the river near the site of this tavern you may still hear the cries of the ghosts of murdered men.

But now let us tell you why this stretch of river will forever be haunted by its past.

The white sarvis trees were in bloom and it was a beautiful day that Spring afternoon of 1864 when Clifford Young rode into the little town of Marshall, North Carolina. Surrounded by steep purple mountains, the homes perched precariously on stilts against the side of the cliff.

The traveler had made up his mind that since there were at least two more hours of daylight, he would seek lodging on the drover's road and stopped to question the first villager he met about a place to stay overnight.

"Wall, I reckon you might say Chunn's Tavern is nearest," the mountaineer replied. "That is if you ain't afeard to stay there."

"Afraid? Why should I be?" asked Young curiously.

"Oh, no reason 'cept them that stays there ain't always heered from again—least not in this world. Some folks says the place is haunted."

Young could hardly refrain from smiling at this bit of mountain credulity, and after asking the distance to the "haunted" hostelry he rode on through town. A few minutes later his horse was trotting cautiously along a steep and rugged path. Ordinarily darkness held little fear for this ex-soldier who had lived through the horrors of the Confederate retreat from Nashville. But as night began to close in around him in this densely wooded hill country, he could not shake off a feeling of apprehension.

His eyes strained to see ahead in the fast deepening

twilight. Heavy undergrowth fringed the trail at either edge and horse and rider seemed to share a sense of dread as they passed through the gloomy depths of the woods.

A shrill cry shattered the stillness. Young started, then reined his mare in more tightly just as she stumbled and almost lost her balance. For a moment the animal stood still, gave a nervous whinny and then continued to climb.

He could only conjecture that the cry had been that of some animal, perhaps a wildcat. But try as he would to suppress such thoughts, Young's mind kept returning the the mountaineer's warning. He could not dispel his depression.

It was in this mood that the finally rounded a bend in the trail and saw Chunn's Tavern for the first time. There it stood, a huge monstrosity of a building, crouched with its back against the mountainside. Across its face ran a long, overhanging porch. Dim strips of light showed through the shuttered windows. And beside the front door hung a perforated metal lantern like a malevolent eye emitting sparks of hate.

Young's first thought was that the tavern's appearance lent itself well to the mountaineer's tale. But he upbraided himself for such foolishness and, dismounting, lifted the large knocker on the door. It was opened almost immediately by a short, heavyset fellow. And with a hearty familiarity which Young found most repellent, the man ushered him in.

"My name is Chunn and we are so delighted, so delighted to have such a gentleman as yourself stop with us," greeted his host unctuously. Chunn's manner and vacuous looking face filled Young with revulsion, but at least his fears were groundless. Certainly, a man of this sort was far too servile to be dangerous. Such a manner was more often found in cowards.

Chunn introduced him to his wife, a scrawny woman with piercing black eyes who preceded him up the stairs and to his room. As it was seven o'clock, Young decided that he would sup in the main room below and come back up to bed immediately thereafter. Tomorrow's ride would be a long one.

The huge fireplace with its blazing logs radiated warmth and made the dining room of the tavern unexpectedly cheerful. Young forgot his somber thoughts of a short while before and gazed curiously around him at the other lodgers.

His eyes fell first on an overdressed, bumptious pair whom he guessed might be a sutler and his wife. Her bonnet was laden with feathers and furbelows and from beneath its brim stared tiny, gimlet eyes made smaller by the puffy folds of flesh around them. Her trader husband was as grossly corpulent as she. And his face looked as if a huge hand had been stroked downward upon it blurring any traces of character it might once have had.

At another table sat a rough looking fellow who still wore the cape style army overcoat of the Union forces. But Young had a suspicion it had been borrowed without leave from some unlucky Yankee. The man was determined to avoid his eye.

The most sensitive and intelligent face belonged to a young man with a russet beard who sat nearest him. His clothes gave off an air of quiet elegance, a bit startling in this isolated mountain area. At this moment the young man arose and walked over to his table.

"I would guess from your bearing, sir, that you

have been a military man. Is that true?"

Replying courteously in the affirmative, Young invited him to join him. His name was Clarkson, and he proved to be a Virginian like himself. One might judge from his dress that he was extremely well-to-do. Young was particularly struck by the heavy gold chain and handsome watch which Clarkson wore.

The two men must have talked for over an hour when they noticed it was getting late and, both wanting to make an early start the following morning, they bid each other the friendliest of good-nights and retired to their own quarters.

As Clifford Young unlocked the door of his room he heard a footstep just behind him. Wheeling around he saw the rough looking fellow he had noticed in the dining room. Still in his army overcoat he scurried past and ducked furtively through a door a short distance down the hall. What was behind the man's strange manner and why had he attempted to avoid his gaze in the dining room?

Young puzzled over it as he lay in his bed leafing through the pages of his Jefferson's Bible. He must have read later than he realized for when he turned down his lamp, it was half after eleven. He had just begun to doze off, comfortable under the warmth of the heavy quilts, when he heard it. His whole body tingled with horror. He heard the sound of a man's screams, screams so fearful that all the dark corners of the mind must have joined hands and forced their way out through a human throat. There was a dull thudding noise and then—silence.

Clifford Young jumped from his bed and as he did so his own lamp flickered out and he found himself in total darkness. For a few seconds he stood tensed, half expecting some intruder to throw himself upon him from the blackness. But nothing happened and finally his fumbling fingers grasped the doorknob. He flung it wide open and there, squarely in front of him, stood Mrs. Chunn, her eyes wide and enigmatic.

"Oh, you are awake, sir. How you did startle me throwing the door open that way."

"Madam, where did that screaming come from?"

"Screaming? I didn't hear anything. Perhaps one of the gentlemen had a nightmare."

As young started to move past her into the hall, the woman stepped almost imperceptibly to one side so that he found his way blocked. For a moment they stood staring at one another. Then, loath to argue with her, Young turned and went back into his room. But there was no sleep left for him that night.

He arose very early and, dressing quickly, ate breakfast and left Chunn's Tavern. Mist still hung over the mountainside making it hard to see any distance ahead. The sharp turn in the trail was upon him before he realized it as he rode along. He heard a crackling sound in the brush but took it to be a fox or a rabbit. Then and utterly without warning came the sharp report of a gun from his right. Recalling a trick he had used to advantage during the war, Young allowed himself to fall from his horse as though hit and his hand came to rest on his revolver.

The figure of a man emerged from a thicket and as it did so Young drew aim and fired. His assailant fell. Leaping to his feet with his revolver still pointed at the figure on the ground he advanced cautiously. To his amazement, he found what appeared to be the body of a dead Negro man. As he turned him over Young saw something glitter in the half light of the early morning. And out of the dead man's pocket fell a gold watch and chain. It was the watch and chain Clarkson had worn the night before.

Anger swept over him like a torrent and his first thought was to get back to the tavern. He rode with the abandon of a madman and wrenching open the door called out to Mrs. Chunn.

"I have just killed the man who murdered Clarkson. What do you know of all this?"

The woman stood stone still, her face ashen.

"My God!" she screamed. "You have killed my husband!" And with that she ran out of the tavern and up the trail.

For the first time the realization of what had actually happened took shape in Clifford Young's mind. He knew now the fate of the guests at the "tavern of terror." His friend, Clarkson, had died at the hands of the Chunns the night before, and prosperous looking guests who were not done away with at the tavern were waylaid on the trail. Where the trail turned made an ideal place to ambush travelers and Chunn, himself, had lain in wait for him that morning, blackening his face as a disguise and attempting to murder him. This time Alfred Chunn had met his match.

His and his wife's game of death with their hapless lodgers was over forever. But for many years afterwards riders along this isolated mountain road often reported hearing wild cries and seeing eerie figures appear suddenly in front of them. It is not surprising, for if the spirits of those who die a violent death are restless and prone to return, there are many with a reason to haunt this road. And, certainly, the evil spirit most likely to wait and watch and linger on out of the past is the ghost of Alfred Chunn himself.

If you should go this way at night, look for him. He may be looking for you.

The Surrency Ghost

A railroad ran special trains for people to watch these strange happenings of the supernatural

It is doubtful whether one person in a thousand driving down Highway 82 through Jessup, Georgia, knows that they are close to the site of one of the strangest supernatural occurrences on record.

Terrifying events took place at the plantation of Millard Surrency despite his reluctance at first to discuss them. From 1872 to 1877, thousands of people visited "Surrency," including scientists bent on explaining away the events and reporters sent from their newspapers to investigate. A railroad even ran special trains for people to watch such predictably regular exhibitions of the supernatural.

One summer afternoon in June of 1872, Mrs. Surrency sat quietly sewing in her bedroom. The beautiful mahogany headboard of the four poster bed gleamed in the light of the sunshine which streamed through the window. Her husband, Millard, was pleased with the stand of cotton on the plantation.

The children were enjoying the swimming, dancing and exchange of visits, all part of the pleasures of summer. Mrs. Surrency could not have been happier. As she sewed a feeling of contentment pervaded her and she didn't notice a noise behind her. It came again and she looked around the room but saw nothing. The third time she realized that it came from the washstand behind her which was near the head of the bed. She stopped her work and gazed at it curiously. To her amazement, the pitcher in the washstand bowl at first almost imperceptibly, then with greater agitation, began to rock back and forth. Gradually enough momentum was generated so that it actually inscribed an arc over the side of the bowl and landed upright beside it on the washstand. Mrs. Surrency was now sure that one of her boys must have tied a string to the pitcher and be playing a trick upon her. She examined the pitcher, but there was no sign of any string.

Ann Surrency was calm of temperament and her first reaction was more that of puzzlement than fear. She had just turned toward the door, wondering where the boys were, when a loud crash came from behind her. Turning she saw the floor in front of the washstand covered with fragments of china and glass. The bowl lay in a thousand fragments at her feet. Pieces of the matching china soap dish were there, too. Even the hand-painted glasses at the back of the stand were now nothing but sharp, silvery slivers along the debris scattered upon the dark floor.

While Mrs. Surrency stood in astonishment gazing at the remains of her once lovely toilet set, she happened to look over at the washstand just as the pitcher began to rise slowly into the air. As if tilted by some invisible hand, it remained poised while the

water it contained was poured slowly out upon the
rug. Then with a kind of savage flourish it was lifted
high and flung to the floor.

Mrs. Surrency ran from the room.

The first person she met was her sixteen-year old
daughter, Clementine, and son, Millard, Jr., who had
come into the large center hall. They were calling her

63

to settle an argument as to who was to ride their father's handsome new stallion, Sea Horse, first. Both hushed quickly when they saw the expression on their mother's face.

She told them what had happened and during the conversation their father came in from his morning tour of the plantation. After some discussion everyone tended to think that the entire incident was probably the result of an earthquake tremor. So they dismissed it from their minds.

The next day as the family were together for their mid-day meal, a door which opened on the long gallery at the side of the house closed with a loud bang. The entire family jumped at the unexpected noise, then agreed that it must have been the wind.

"Perhaps we are going to have a summer storm," said Mr. Surrency, folding his napkin. As he did so the Surrencys heard the same heavy door creak open and close with such a violent crash that it almost shook the house. Young Millard pointed speechless at two of the dining room windows. The two windows which had been raised were now edging downward simultaneously. They struck the sills and began to go back up faster until as they opened and closed loudly several times some of the small panes were shattered.

Clementine began to cry. Her mother tried to sooth her. Young Millard went over to check the windows while Millard Surrency, Sr., and his older brother Robert ran out of the dining room toward the gallery. They could see no one, and a thorough search of the grounds near the home revealed nothing.

Entering the separate kitchen back of the house, Mr. Surrency found the family butler and cook. Both looked extremely frightened. Maggie literally shook, and the pair seemed as puzzled by the racket as the Surrencys.

This was only the beginning. From then on many strange and frightening incidents took place, although they seemed to be restricted to Mrs. Surrency's bedroom or the dining room. On several occasions the family sat down to a beautifully set table and appetizing meal and before there was sufficient time for the family to bow their head for the blessing, the table cloth with the serving dishes, plates, crystal and everything upon it would be snatched from the table. The food was unceremoniously dumped into the Surrency's laps and on the floor.

Even when the Surrency's meals stayed on the table there was a continual succession of other minor, although sometimes painful, disasters. Hot tea, coffee, or soup was often flung in the faces of various members of the family. Their forks or spoons sometimes broke in two or were twisted out of shape even as they held them in their hands.

It was not long before the events, first confined to Mrs. Surrency's bedroom and the dining room, began to spread throughout the house. Doors and windows would slam, furniture would begin to move in an eerie dance about the room, then back to its place, or fall forward with a crash which sometimes shattered valuable family pieces. There was an ever-present danger for the children as heavy wardrobes and bureaus tended to suddenly topple forward, and mirrors and pictures frequently fell from the walls.

These weird phenomena went on during the night as well as the day until the entire family barely ate or slept, awaiting the next shocking event.

For some reason the manifestations seemed to single out young Clementine for the most lurid and dramatic demonstrations. If she touched a table, when she withdrew her hand the table followed her, floating along perhaps a foot above the floor. If she sat in a chair, when she arose the chair would trail her throughout the house. It was a strange sight indeed to watch Clementine Surrency go down the stairs, through the house and out to the garden with a chair floating right along just a few feet behind her.

Even worse, it became so that Clementine could scarcely enter the room without all the furniture lifting from the floor and engaging in a weird, maniacal kind of dance, whirling here and there for as long as five minutes at a time, until suddenly all became still. Or one would crash with incredible ferocity into another, wrecking some beautiful family heirloom.

The Surrencys discussed moving to another plantation which Mr. Surrency owned, but they had spent many happy years in this house built in the 1840's and they were reluctant to leave.

Mrs. Surrency became increasingly alarmed over the physical safety of the children and that of Clementine in particular. Invisible hands would tug her hair roughly, her bedclothes were snatched from the bed. Sometimes as the girl was about to go to sleep, her bed would begin to rock violently to and fro as if attempting to throw her out of it. Early one morning in February, she was lifted entirely out of bed just before the incredibly heavy canopied bed was overturned, falling sideways on the floor with a horrendous crash which awakened the entire household.

That day the family made up their minds that they would move to the other plantation as soon as they could pack their belongings, a matter of a few days. But the move was not destined to be made in so leisurely a fashion. For that very afternoon the danger of the malevolent force at work in the Surrency house showed itself most clearly. As young Sam Surrency walked into the library where his brother Robert sat quietly reading in a chair before the fire, he saw one of the huge brass andirons lift itself from the flames into the air. For a moment it poised itself as if gathering every possible ounce of force. Then the massive andiron hurled itself through the air in the direction of Robert's head who sat unsuspecting in the chair. Before Sam could reach him the andiron had dealt Robert a glancing blow on the head. Sam tried to grasp the andiron but it was wrested from his hands and again struck Robert. This time the boy ran for his life. But the andiron followed, striking him viciously until he fell unconscious to the floor in a pool of blood. The andiron then rose into the air and, moving down the wide center hall, re-entered the library and settled itself back in the fireplace.

That evening the Surrencys, with the help of friends, moved Robert and the rest of the family to the other plantation, closing the old homeplace and taking only their clothes. The other house was furnished also and in addition there was the thought in each one's mind that the old furniture was unwelcome in new surroundings. Robert's wounds became infected and illness followed.

For almost two weeks the emotionally exhausted Surrencys recovered from the habit of jumping at every slight sound, not knowing what would soon follow. Broken limbs, wounds and bruises healed. Many of these latter were suffered by the children who had been caught beneath falling cabinets, wardrobes, et cetera.

But emotional stability had only begun to return

67

when all the nightmarish events descended upon them again. For a few days the family did not talk about it with outsiders, but they soon became desperate. As word of the Surrency ghost spread many distinguished people came to investigate such as Bridges Smith, Mayor of Macon, and Henry Pendleton, Editor of the Macon *Telegram*. Many reliable people, neighbors who lived near Jessup, Georgia, saw these weird phenomena take place.

Finally, the well-known medium and clairvoyant of the day, Foster, visited the Surrency home with some of his friends and remained for a week investigating. He reported that he had been in contact with spirits who told him the entire Surrency family was strongly mediumistic, especially Clementine. These were the type of people, said Foster, which spirits sought out to convey their messages to others. The Surrency family took little stock in Foster's explanation.

Shortly after their troubles began in their new home, Millard Surrency started building a small house on another piece of property he owned. When they were ready to move, he gave in to Clementine's pleadings to visit their old home so that she might pack up some of her belongings which she had left in the family's hasty move.

While Clementine packed her trunk in the house her father walked around looking at the grounds once more. Soon Clementine returned telling him her trunk was ready to be brought down. Even as she spoke there came the sound of crashing glass. The trunk hurtled through the closed window and shutters and fell on the lawn near them. The lid had burst open and the girl's clothes, in wild disarray, were spilling over the side and out on the lawn. And they were literally torn to shreds.

68

"We mustn't ever come here again," cried Clementine. She clung to her father sobbing hysterically.

"This house must certainly be cursed by some unspeakable evil," said Surrency. And from that day on none of the Surrency family ever returned. For over 45 years the house sat deserted until it finally burned.

The problems of the family ended after they moved into their new home which founded the small community of Surrency, Georgia. But the frightening phenomena which had plagued the family for so long were never solved and for years the people of nearby Jessup, who had actually seen the weird events taking place, continued to talk of them. Many had been eye witnesses to incidents which so completely violated human understanding they could only conjecture a force was at work which was in no way bound by natural laws. And to this day the ghost of Surrency has never been explained.

The King's Messengers

On rainy nights the eerie pair still roam, galloping along forever carrying a message never to be delivered

Major Ferguson leaned back against the white oak tree and reflected upon his situation.

His proclamation for the mountain men to surrender may have been flamboyant, but he never really expected it to create this kind of reaction. Hundreds of men were appearing as if by magic from over the mountains, traveling under the command of Campbell, Shelby, Sevier and others from that almost mythical land beyond Quaker Meadows, even beyond the edge of his map. They were coming to do battle with him. They were coming down to the lowlands to fight for their independence and there was an understanding among them that they would not go home until either they or Ferguson had been defeated.

For several days now he had been sending out his messengers in pairs, two by two, to alert Lord Cornwallis at his headquarters in Charlottesburg as to the situation. Not that his position on King's Mountain was that precarious, but he wouldn't have minded a regiment of the king's dragoons close enough to support him.

Ordinarily Major Ferguson was not the kind of man to worry, but somehow messengers were not getting through to Lord Cornwallis and in the cold chill of the October wind, he sensed the hostility of these backwoods people who refused to bow to the British flag or—what was more important—pay taxes.

The day before he had sent some of his best riders off but still there was no return message from Lord

Cornwallis. No need to waste any more of his good men on futile errands. Tonight he would send a couple of the Tory militia. He would select natives of the area, roughly dressed. They certainly would not get lost and if they ran into any mountain men, they'd be instant turncoats for as long as it took to get off down the road.

James and Douglas Duncan were farm born and bred. Unlettered but fairly shrewd fellows, their greatest loyalty was to their possessions and the protection the British flag might give their land.

Ferguson summoned the two brothers and gave them this most vital message instructing them to deliver it in person to Lord Rawdon or Lord Cornwallis at Charlottesburg. He warned them about the hazards of their mission, told them of the messengers who had not gotten through, cautioned them to talk to no one and then dispatched the nondescript pair on horseback.

For some time they rode along on this cold, rainy October night, meeting neither friend nor foe. After they had galloped for a number of miles without incident, they reached the South Fork of the Catawba River. They plunged the animals into the stream and with a great splashing and whinnying they forded the river. The men were relieved to find a tavern there at which to refresh themselves.

The tavern mistress had just lost her husband at the battle of Camden and the two sympathized with her volubly. So much so that she generously made their drinks extra hearty and as their tongues loosened, their braggadoccio remarks began to arouse the woman's suspicions that here were two Tories bent on mischief of some kind. Seeing they were almost ready to leave she slipped out of the room and up to the attic of the tavern where she stood by the window waiting. Their horses were tethered just below her and she knew the direction they would ride in. She had just taken out a brace of pistols when the two drunken couriers appeared below her, mounted their horses and rode off. Taking aim she fired the first shot at the one on the right. Nothing happened. The other pistol fired a second later at the rider on the left. But neither man fell and the two riders galloped on, disappearing down the muddy road and into the night.

It was nearing four o'clock in the morning when innkeeper Amos Bissell near Salisbury heard a rough pounding at the door and, awakening, looked down to see what guests could be arriving at this hour on such a cold and rainy night. It was pitch black and, unable to see anyone, all he could hear was what appeared to be the loud voices of two men raised in anger.

"We should have taken a path toward the east hours ago. You don't know the way after all, you simpleton!"

"This is the way that varmint of a woman said to go."

"Well, drat her miserable Whig soul. Her advice is as worthless as the Continental Congress."

The two men lit a lantern and brought out a large map which they spread upon a tree stump. Now the innkeeper could see their horses. One man held the lantern while the other appeared to be studying it.

"We'd better ask the way again. Charlottesburg can't be fur from here," Bissell heard one of the men say.

He threw a long coat on over his nightshirt and unlocking the door to his room, picked his way carefully down the steep curving staircase, candle in hand. He stopped to pick up a flintlock pistol, just as a precaution, and began to walk carefully around the sleeping forms of his guests who lay stretched out on the floor around the fireplace.

Slipping back the heavy iron bolt on the Inn door he peered out. There was no one there. Drawing the coat more tightly around him, he ventured a few feet from the Inn, and then around the corner of the building growing increasingly curious, but he still saw nothing at all nor did he hear even the slightest sound. The rain had stopped but the ground was soft and soggy. Going over to the large tree stump where he had seen the two men spread out the map, Bissell scrutinized the ground around it thoroughly looking for prints of boots and horses' hooves. But not only was the yard of the Inn deserted, there was not a mark to be found. A strange chill began at the back of Amos Bissell's neck and traveled the length of his spine. He was just as frightened as he could be and he scurried quickly back into the Inn, bolted the front door and leaned his back against it. His heart was beating so rapidly he rested there a moment until he could compose himself.

Nor was this the last time the two riders were seen. Travelers on the road between Salisbury and Charlotte often saw the riders. Sometimes they were traveling away from their destination. One stage-coach driver said he had "given them directions so many times that he was beginning to resent the delays every time he met them."

Particularly wherever the road forked, the forms of the two couriers were often seen huddled together looking at their map to decide which fork to take. And anyone who chanced by was always hailed and asked the way to Charlottesburg.

"We must be there by morning," one of the men

would invariably say.

Drivers of the stagecoaches found that their horses became fidgety and nervous when approaching the riders, as if they sensed the two shadowy figures no longer belonged to the natural world.

So, as time went on and the war was finally won and the last British soldiers departed for their homeland, the king's messengers became couriers without an army. On rainy nights the eerie pair still roamed, galloping along forever with a message never to be delivered, the writer of the message long since dead and buried in the red earth of King's Mountain.

Settlements grew into towns, then cities, and the two riders became wary of the main roads, taking to the country lanes in their endless search for the way to Charlottesburg.

Some say you can still see them. A cold, rainy night in early October is the best time to look for the King's Messengers. For then they are most apt to suddenly appear galloping over the hill on some lonely dirt road between King's Mountain and Salisbury, two specters hurtling through the night on their phantom steeds, pausing sporadically to inquire the way to Charlottesburg. And, if by chance they should ask you, it doesn't really matter in which direction you point for even with the best of directions an invisible power thwarts and diverts the restless apparitions at every turn.

The Haunted Gold Mine

*The Carolina Gold Rush could have made
him the richest main the world until a ghost
stepped in*

They called him "Skinflint" MacIntosh and said if
you happened to pass him sideways you couldn't see
him. It was kind of a local joke in every country store
between Charlotte and Concord that the only way
you could see MacIntosh was from the front or back.

Not only skinny in size, he also happened to be
skinny when it came to generosity, or at least that's
what everyone said. But the old man was not con-
cerned over what was said about him at the country
stores or jokes about his appearance, for he owned
the richest hill of gold between the Reed Mine and the
United States Mint at Charlotte.

It may have looked like just another field of red
clay on top but when MacIntosh got the report that
the vein of gold 450 feet down was four feet wide, it
brought the only kind of joy a mind like his could
truly appreciate.

Of course, there was a problem. Even with the
shaft dug he must persuade enough men to go down
that far and dig in the damp darkness beneath the

surface of the earth and haul out his treasure. There
were plenty of fellows to be had for placer mining on
the surface. This needed men with more skill and
more courage.

But Mr. MacIntosh was unworried. He knew how
to do it. He sat on his hill and looked at the broom-
straw, a warm, rusty color in the flow of the setting
sun. He picked up a lump of red clay, pressing and
shaping it between his fingers, and he could picture

shovel after shovel full of that red clay turning to pure gold!

It seemed hard to believe that he had been picked, perhaps, he thought, by God himself, to become the richest man in North Carolina. Why, someday people would still be talking about the gold that came out of his mine long after they had forgotten mines like the Dixie Queen, the New Nugget and the Yellow Dog. What if the Reed Mine had been the first mine in this country to gain fame and start the Carolina gold rush, his mine would outproduce them all!

The next morning Mr. MacIntosh went to the store at Georgeville where he knew he would find not only some experienced miners from the Reed Mine but also newly arrived young men who had flocked into the area eager to make their fortunes. Standing there resting one hand on the counter and smiling his friendliest smile, Mr. MacIntosh announced he would pay half again whatever the other mine operators were paying.

"You'll have to," said Joe McGee sitting back with his chair tilted against the counter. "Who wants to go that far down to dig? No amount a' money is worth workin' for if a man don't come up at the end of the day to collect." There was a sizzling sound as he spat at the stove.

For a moment MacIntosh sensed that something could go wrong. There was his fortune and he was willing to pay high wages for men to dig it up for him but somehow these men were not jumping at his offer. Was his mine any different from the others? He alone knew it was the richest. The hairs rose along the back of his neck and for no longer than it takes a snake to flick its tongue, MacIntosh felt cold enough to shiver. There was even a flash of foreboding, but it didn't last long.

"Come up at the end of the day to collect. What are

The Mecklenburg Iron Works made the counter balance
weights now rusting on the hill over Little Meadow Creek—
site of the first gold strike in America. This land is now a
National Historic Landmark, one of only about a dozen in
North Carolina. The Department of Archives and History
hopes to open the property to the public after the restoration
of the old Reed Mine, the first commercial gold mine in
America.

you talkin'' about, Joe? It don't matter how deep a mine is. Whether it's two hundred or three hundred feet under the ground. You just brace the roofs of those tunnels up with good, hefty timber and you dig out the gold the same way. I've been down in that mine myself many a time and I've got the finest oak timbers and braces money can buy."

Mr. MacIntosh knew that was a lie even as he said it. But he smiled his biggest smile again and said, "All right, men, sign up over here, all of you who want to go to work for me Monday morning and start getting rich."

Joe McGee leaned back against the counter and said, "Mr. MacIntosh, if you got the safest mine like you say you have, and I got no reason to doubt you, then there's no danger workin' in your mine."

"That's right," replied MacIntosh. "Why, you're just about as safe down there as a man could be."

"All right," said Joe, I'll come to work for you."

Everyone was surprised because they knew that Joe was probably the best foreman at the Reed Mine and he knew the mining business well.

"But, Mr. MacIntosh, there's just one thing. You wouldn't mind paying my wife a thousand dollars if I did happen to get buried down there in your mine, would you?"

"Joe, I wouldn't pay your wife just one thousand dollars. I'd pay her two thousand!"

Well, that did it. Two thousand dollars was more money than most of the men had ever seen. Joe quit the Reed Mine that afternoon and told the boss he was leaving to work for MacIntosh. At least a dozen other men did the same thing because on the following Monday there was almost a full crew ready to go down into the MacIntosh Mine.

Soon large quantities of ore were being brought up and MacIntosh's excitement was so great these first few weeks that he even treated some of the men to a free drink in the local saloon.

The yield per ton of pure gold, after the Chilean mill had done its work, was incredibly high, it was said, but MacIntosh never told anyone exactly what the yield per ton was. Some of the men were finding sizeable gold nuggets. But most of the gold was found in fissure veins of quartz. This quartz was seldom glassy but rather milky white in color and often stained brown.

On his first payday Joe bought his wife a pair of fine silk stockings. She still worried about him and at first he had to reassure her almost daily. Finally, when he told her how safe the mine was, he would laugh and with his blue green eyes dancing mischievously, remind her that, "Why, if anything did happen to me you'd be rich, lassie! Old MacIntosh promised me himself that you would get two thousand dollars."

So, as the weeks passed and Joe returned safely each night to the little house where his wife, and then a baby as well, awaited him, her fears eased.

But, on the evening of the winter's first snowfall,

Joe did not come home at the accustomed time. It had been a cold, gray, drizzly afternoon with the fine rain turning into snow and Jennie's spirits were low. But she counted this due to the weather remembering that sometimes on a cold day, Joe would stop off with his friend Shaun O'Hennessy and buy a drink, so she refused to worry.

However, by nine o'clock she was quite alarmed. Wrapping the baby warmly, she left the infant with her neighbor and set out toward the saloon. She saw lights inside, laughter drifted out into the snow-flecked blackness and when she opened the door she was engulfed in the warm air, tobacco smoke and voices.

Tommy McSwain, the owner, walked over to her immediately. "What can I do for you, Jennie McGee?" But he was unable to answer any questions about Joe.

"No, mam. Last time Joe was in here was three nights ago. Seems like he and Shaun came in after work. Yes, that's the way it was."

"Anybody seen Joe McGee?" he called out to the men, a number of whom were looking curiously at Jennie by now, for it was plain to see she was upset.

There was a chorus of no's and Jennie left, deciding she would walk on beyond the saloon to Shaun O'Hennessy's. Mary opened the door and she could see Shaun dozing before the fire. He got up stiffly from his chair when he heard the door close behind her.

"What are you doing out at this time of night, my girl? Where is Joe? I waited for him this afternoon, but he said he was going to work awhile longer so I came on home. This back of mine's been hurtin' somethin' terrible."

"Jennie, what's wrong with you," said Shaun's

wife, Mary.

Tears streamed down Jennie's face but at first there was no sound. Then she flung herself into Mary's arms weeping and screaming.

"He's still down there. I know he is. He's had an accident or he'd be home by now. Get him out, Shaun, get him out! *Please!* Go down to the mine tonight."

"Mary, take her home and stay with her until I come and pick you up."

O'Hennessy pulled on his still wet boots which sat beside the fire, reached for his coat and hat which hung on a wooden peg near the door, and left.

Near the saloon he met Big Pete and they rounded up several other men to join them. The mine was only a little over a mile away but the snow made walking more treacherous and the little knot of silent miners tramped along through the blackness punctuated here and there by pinpoints of light from miners' cabins.

Three men passed, arms linked, singing a bawdy song at the top of their lungs. The one nearest Shaun jostled him roughly and if it had been any other time he would have regretted it for Shaun's Irish temper would certainly have blazed up. But his face grew just a shade more grim and he pressed on, ignoring the fellow.

It was cold and raw and the road underfoot which led up the hill to the mine was muddy. But there were stars out and it had begun to clear. The men trudged on, their heavy boots making a scrunching sound on the pieces of quartz and dark greenish gray rocks which lay along the roadbed.

Finally, they reached the place where the mine shaft lay and Shaun and one of the other men, each with their lanterns, started down the ladder and, with the light from the lanterns flickering on the sides of the shaft hewed deep into the red clay, down, down they went, past the gaping holes of old tunnels worked in bygone years and on to the vein the men were working now.

The two men walked the full length of the tunnel where they had worked that day and for the past several months. They called and then they listened. But there was no sound save the muffled echo of their own voices and the scraping of their boots on granite-like rock. After they had searched fruitlessly for about an hour they went back up to the surface where the small huddle of miners who had accompanied them waited.

The next day Jennie went to MacIntosh's office still certain that Joe was somewhere within the mine and asked him to send a search party to comb some of the lesser worked tunnels. Four of the men including Shaun accompanied her, but MacIntosh pooh-poohed the plan and said Joe would show up again "when he gets good and ready." Two weeks passed and still there was no sign of Joe so Jennie, convinced of Joe's devotion to her, was certain by now that the was dead. She visited MacIntosh again, this time to make claim for the two thousand dollars he had promised to pay if Joe were killed in the mine. MacIntosh suggested this time that perhaps Joe had not been so happy with married life, but to wait awhile longer. By now, Jennie and the baby were low on food and firewood and the other miners and their wives were taking by whatever food they could to share and Shaun O'Hennessy was chopping fire-wood for his own family and Jennie as well.

The next time Jennie went to the mine office MacIntosh sent a message out that he did not have

time to see her. In tears she stopped by the

In the picture are Chilean grinding stones and an old stone chimney on the Reed property recently purchased by the state of North Carolina. This property had been designated a National Historic Landmark in the mid-sixties but not until the purchase of the land in the Spring of 1971 was it certain that the first gold mine in America would be restored and preserved.

O'Hennessy shack on her way home and Mary O'Hennessy made her stay on for some hot stew. Over and over she kept moaning, "He's dead, he's dead. He's down there somewhere dead. What will the baby and I do now."

That night it had barely struck twelve when there came a terrible rattling sound at the O'Hennessy door. Shaun pulled on his trousers and stumbled toward it sleepily. Without thinking he threw the door wide open and then he wished he had not, for before him stood the most frightful figure he had ever seen. The cheeks were a waxy chalk white. The eyes in their dark caverns looked like murky red marbles. Gaunt, clothes encrusted all over with dirt, one could hardly tell that it was a man.

Shaun covered his eyes in horror. A voice spoke.

"Ah, Shaun O'Hennessy. You were the best friend I had in all the world, and now you will not even look on me. Are you going to leave me down in the dark and the damp of the mine forever? And what about Jennie? Is old 'Skinflint' going to pay her the money for my life? What about your Mary? And the rest of the wives. Do you ken he will do any the better by them? Look at me, Shaun."

O'Hennessy lowered his arm slowly from before his eyes and peered at the specter of his old friend. For this weird spirit in front of him had once been Joe McGee.

"I heard you the night you came to look for me, Shaun, but you went down too deep. Stop at the second tunnel and go in. If you'll walk far enough, you'll find me. That's where I decided to stop and work for awhile the day I didn't go out with you. I was striking rich ore when the timber gave way and buried me. But none of that matters now. Has

MacIntosh given Jennie any money?"

"No, he won't give it to her, Joe."

"Won't give it to her! Well, blast him! Why not?"

"Says you ain't dead, Joe. Just went off and left her."

The ghost flew into a terrible rage and as brave a man as he was, Shaun O'Hennessy began to tremble.

"The liar! The greedy old devil! I'll haunt that mine of his forever," shouted the specter. Then he began to calm down somewhat when he saw the effect all this was having on his friend.

"Now, Shaun. You ain't scared of your old buddy Joe, are you? I want you to get Big Pete, Casey, Henry and Sam and come after me."

"Yeah, yeah. Tomorrow morning. We'll be there, Joe."

"No, not tomorrow morning. Tonight!" and with that the ghost vanished.

Still shaking, Shaun pulled on his boots and left. He knew he was not going down into that mine alone. He made four stops and each miner came with him after he told them about seeing Joe's ghost. Tonight there was moonlight and it seemed to Shaun that they reached the mine quickly, almost too quickly. The men were jumpy and uneasy but they were determined to find out if the specter had really been the ghost of Joe McGee. Single file they went down the ladder.

Casey walked along in front of the others watching for holes in the floor of the tunnel or loose overhead timbers. They had walked for perhaps two hundred feet when a voice spoke up and said, "I've been waiting for you, boys," and there stood the specter, white-faced, hollow-eyed and clothes encrusted with dirt.

"It's time you knew old MacIntosh is one of the

87

worst liars there ever was. This mine ain't safe and it never will be because them's cheap timbers and a lot of 'em are even rotten. I'm goin' to haunt this mine forever!"

The miners looked terrified but Shaun and Big Pete stood their ground behind Sam and Casey.

"Dig here?" asked Casey.

"Yes," replied the ghost, pointing toward the cave-in. "Why, I've walked all over this mine lately, watchin' you fellows, fearin' for you."

The frightened men dug for almost ten minutes. They were beginning to grow discouraged when there was a ring as Big Pete's shovel struck metal.

The metal turned out to be a pick and the handle of the pick was clutched fast in a man's fist. Shaun and Big Pete dropped their shovels and began to dig with their hands now. Within minutes they had uncovered the body of a man and the man was Joe McGee. No one thought to notice when the ghost disappeared because no one had really wanted to keep looking at it.

They carried Joe's body up on the elevator and home, and the next morning Shaun went to get MacIntosh. He told him Joe McGee was home and "needed to see him and he'd better come."

Mr. MacIntosh looked pretty startled, like he was going to call Shaun down, but instead he decided to go with him. Neither man did any talking on the walk from the mine office over to the McGee shack. There was a crow of miners standing around outside the little house looking sullen and silent. Three women were standing on the porch talking and MacIntosh made his way through several more who were gathered just outside the front door.

Shaun held the door open and Mr. MacIntosh walked in. At one end of the room was a long pine box and MacIntosh knew even before he walked over to it that Joe McGee lay inside the crude coffin. Jennie sat in the small rocker next to it holding the baby and crying quietly. She did not look up at MacIntosh.

A thousand dollars, that's what it was, wasn't it," said MacIntosh. Jennie didn't answer.

An angry murmur rose from the men.

"Two thousand, " broke in Big Pete. "You know what it is. We was there in the store the day you hired him. We know how often Jennie's been to you to get it."

MacIntosh started toward the door and the men gradually closed the way in front of him until he found himself looking up into the angry face of Pete Petroni whom everybody knew was not called "Big Pete" for nothing. He tried to go around him. "Big Pete" moved blocking his exit.

"All right, two thousand," he said gruffly. "She can pick it up at the mine office."

That afternoon Mary O'Hennessy went with Jennie to pick up her money and it was paid.

But the men did not go back to work that day, nor did they go back the next. Skinflint called an "important meeting" of all the miners. They all came and listened. He promised more money, he bragged about the safety of the mine and he said he had just forgotten how much Joe's wife was to get and that he was so sorry about it he had even given her fifty dollars more.

The men heard him out, their faces impassive. Then they got up and left. But the next morning there was still no sign of life at the mine and he learned that all of the men, except for a few who were packing to leave the area, had hired on at other nearby mines. Word had spread quickly that the MacIntosh mine was haunted, that it always would be, and when that kind of news gets out a mine operator is finished.

For several days MacIntosh visited some of the leaders among the men trying to convince them to go back but they wouldn't even talk with him. Finally, he gave up.

A few weeks later he walked up the hill and began to wander around aimlessly. He looked regretfully at the tall rock smelting furnace from which no smoke had come for days. He sat down at the edge of the huge grinding stones and sifted crushed quartz aimlessly through his fingers as if in a daze.

He had sat this way for perhaps an hour when a mounting fury began to overtake him. His dream of a lifetime was to be destroyed because of some superstitious miners. There was millions of dollars of gold in this hill, but he was never going to see it. He knew it. Somehow there must be a way to get it out.

And then, like an animal gone mad and with tears of frustration streaming down his face, he began to claw at the red clay with his fingers. MacIntosh was not the first man to lose his mind over gold.

A hundred years later the gold is still there. The miners have all left and no one would know that beneath the red clay of these Carolina hills the best and the worst in man struggled with each other in the search for gold.

If you should walk across these hills, you may still hear the wind whispering the names of these mines—the Dixie Queen, the Yellow Dog, the Blue Hill, The Dutch Bend and the Reed Mine, but even the wind does not mention the name of the MacIntosh Mine.

The Singing River

*Is it possible that there are lost Indian tribes
who went to live beneath the water?*

Late summer and autumn are the times when the
mysterious music of the Pascagoula River is heard
most often, and those who have listened to it remember it forever. Some say it is a soft humming sound,
others hear the strains of music so beautiful that it is
unearthly. Those who have heard it most clearly
have been out in a boat on the river itself rather than
the bank and have heard the strains of the music
begin gently around them and then swell louder and
louder. They were caught up and carried along by
the power and beauty of the strange melody which
yet contained a prevailing note of sadness.

Located on U.S. 90 between Biloxi, Mississippi and
Mobile, Alabama, the river is named for the Pascagoula Indians who lived along its banks, and for
many years a variety of legends has attempted to
explain the music.

One of the best known of these legends is the story
of the romance between Princess Anola who was
betrothed to the chieftain of the warlike Biloxi Indians and young Altama, son of the Pascagoula chief.
The tribe of the Pascagoula was known for their

friendly, peaceful ways and unlike some of the other Indian tribes, war never became a pastime with them. Although not as warlike as some, they did not escape that desire for vengeance which started so many Indian wars and even destroyed entire tribes.

The Pascagoulas held their feasts, their rhythmic dances, their burial ceremonies as did all the Indians but for the most part they were content to cultivate the ground with their primitive hooked wooden sticks, planting corn and beans and living in relative peace with their neighbors.

War was far from the minds of Anola and Altama when they first came upon each other in the forest near the Pascagoula village. Altama was quietly fishing in the river when he first heard something more than the normal sound of the water. It was the voice of a girl singing softly and blending with the noises of the forest and stream.

Altama searched the woods all around him but could find no one. Then he gazed up through the branches of the tree right over his head and there, perched among the highest limbs, was a lovely girl. He beckoned to her to come down and the two spent the balance of the afternoon sharing each other's thoughts and dreams. It was the first of many meetings and Altama soon convinced the girl to marry him.

So, one day she left the village of her father and was welcomed warmly by the people of Altama who immediately began to busy themselves preparing the elaborate wedding feast ordered by Altama's father. On the afternoon before the day of the feast a lone Pascagoula brave was out hunting some distance from the village when he heard the sound of voices talking in the Biloxi tongue. He concealed himself well and stood watching while hosts of Biloxi braves

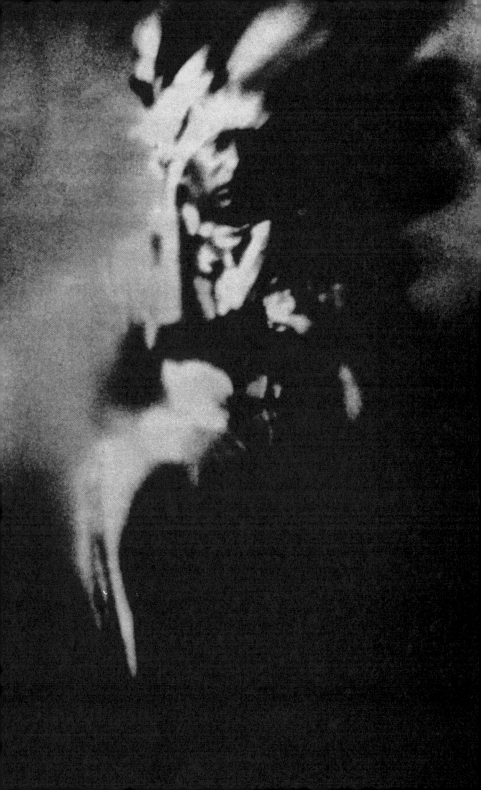

in war regalia stole quietly past him traveling in the direction of the Pascagoula village. It was not hard for the hunter to guess that their objective was vengeance upon the Pascagoula for the loss of their angry chieftain's betrothed.

The hunter returned speedily to his tribe with news of the impending disaster, for those whom the Biloxi did not kill, they would surely take as slaves. Altama volunteered to go out alone to meet the Biloxi and offer himself to them in an attempt to save the village, but the other braves would not allow him to do this.

Soon the scout they had sent out to confirm the hunter's story returned. He brought news of many Biloxi warriors on the march, far outnumbering the Pascagoula braves, warriors who would soon descend with warlike screams and cries upon the villagers. A brief council was held and the people chose between death and slavery at the hands of the Biloxi or another alternative—the waters of their beloved river. They made their decision and gathering along the banks the old people and children began to walk out into the dark stream. They were followed by the braves chanting a death song and behind them walked Altama and Anola who embraced and then plunged beneath the swift flowing waters.

When the Biloxi arrived they found burning campfires and preparations for an elaborate wedding feast. But all was deathly still, nor was there any sign of man, woman or child anywhere about. It was a strange scene and there was something so eerie about it that even seasoned warriors found themselves tiptoeing about, looking in the doorways of the small cabins, staring at the smoking meat and warm vessels of food suspiciously if not fearfully. After making certain no one was there, they left, much mystified.

From that day on stories have been told of the "singing river," and of the people who chose death rather than slavery. The rippling, poignant song of the river has been heard down through the years and continues to puzzle those who seek to explain everything by the laws of science.

Interestingly enough, this is only one of a number of Indian stories of strange sounds coming from rivers and other bodies of water. The white man dreams of lost cities which continue to exist below the water and the Indian appears to have dreams buried deep in his memory of lost tribes and warriors who went to live beneath the water. Many of their stories mention songs of sadness or revelry still heard by those who are fortunate and perceptive enough.

As modern man considers building cities on the ocean floor one sometimes wonders whether in the dawn of mankind men were able to live underwater as well as on land and whether these legends dredged up from the dim recesses of men's minds are really remnants of his prehistoric past.

In any event, if you visit the Pascagoula River in the late summer or autumn you may be one of those who will hear the weird and plaintive song of the water, and then you can decide what it is and why it is there.

The Gray Lady

She walks across the barriers of time to warn the living

Few there are who have not heard the story of the Gray Man of Pawley's Island, South Carolina. He walks the sandy strand of that island to warn inhabitants of impending hurricanes.

But less known is the story of another South Carolina ghost called the Gray Lady and that is a shame. For she walks not on the sands of the shore but from out of the mist of history at the edge of men's minds. She walks as does the Gray Man to carry a warning from the dead to the living, a warning of impending danger and the possibility of assistance.

She first appeared to save the life of her brother, bringing the garments of a monk which enabled him to disguise himself and escape the St. Bartholomew's Day massacre. That was in France four hundred years ago and from time to time after that she appeared to descendants or intimates of the De Saurin family.

It is strange that such an old ghost should appear so young to those who see her. That a ghost could be both beautiful and frightening at the same time is not only possible—it is, it has been and it may be again for there is no proof that she has left South Carolina.

Nina Beaumont knew little about the De Saurin family in Camden when Raoul De Saurin, whom she had consented to marry, invited her there almost a century ago. It was Halloween and a gay party was assembled in one of the beautifully furnished rooms of "Lausanne," the name the family had given to their home. Among the paintings of her future husband's ancestors was one of a lovely girl in the garb of a nun. The face was infinitely sad and somehow Nina's gaze kept returning to it. She began to question Raoul about the nun and his reluctance to talk about her was soon apparent.

"It is such a wild and rainy night outside and so cheerful in this room that I want only to talk about happy things," said Raoul gently.

But this just aroused Nina's curiosity further and other members of the party joined in, begging him to tell the story. Finally, he consented.

"The name of the girl was Eloise De Saurin and she had been confined to a convent by her father to prevent her from marrying a young man who was not of her faith. The convent where he placed her was one of the most severe of the day and after she had spent only a year there Eloise died. Her death was followed shortly afterwards by that of her grieving mother. The father, Darce De Saurin, in a moment of guilt and despair, took his own life. His two sons whom he had banished because of their Protestant sympathies were summoned and arrived in time to hear his confession. He claimed that he had seen Eloise herself and his belief that she had come to reproach him led him to stab himself with the same dagger with which he had threatened the life of the

young man she loved."

"The story goes that later she appeared to the brothers, who recognized her instantly, and she left the garments in which my namesake, Raoul, was to escape being massacred. Jules did not escape and was murdered."

"So," said Raoul, "her appearances, according to family tradition, have happened each time before some tragic event in our family. She has always been seen by some member of the family and with the same expression of sorrow. But so far she has not deigned to visit any of us," he said, smiling and making light of the whole story.

The Court Inn at Camden, South Carolina where the Gray Lady was last seen is no longer standing

99

Nina, however, could not smile for her good spirits had fled and she felt both depressed and apprehensive. After the guests left she and Raoul stayed to talk awhile longer. Then she went up to her room. Try as she would to go to sleep, she could not, so, throwing on a robe, she decided to go down the hall and see if Raoul's sister was still awake. She took the candle holder from her bedside table and started down the dark hall which was illuminated dimly by the moonlight coming in the window at the end of the hall.

The hall was quite dark but she was able to make out the figure of a woman only a few feet ahead of her. Thinking it was Lucia, Nina called out gaily. But there was no response. They grayclad figure continued on its way down the hall just in front of her and now, she noticed that rather than walk, it appeared to glide! Who was this strange woman? Her diaphanous robes and shimmering veil lent a supernatural effect both frightening and intriguing. Nina was almost upon her when the woman turned and looked directly at her. The face was young and lovely but filled with sadness. To her amazement she recognized the features as those of the nun in the painting.

The nun gazed at her with tears streaming down her face and clasped her hands as if imploring her for help. Before she could recover herself enough to know what to do, the veiled figure began to grow dim and melted away like a cloud blown before the wind. Afterwards Nina could not remember whether her candle had blown out or how she had gotten back to her room.

She awoke to find herself still in her robe lying across the bed. And although it was a bright and beautiful day she was filled with foreboding. The face of the nun was etched sharply and clearly upon her consciousness and even if she was unable to understand the events of the night, she felt that it had been a warning, if not for her, for someone she loved. At breakfast she ate little and when Raoul began to talk about the hunt planned for that day she became very upset and begged him not to go. Finally, she told him why and he began to laugh, surprised that she could be so superstitious as to believe in an old legend. Between his affectionate reassurances and some teasing, he quieted her fears so that she waved and managed to smile at him as he rode off to hunt with his friends.

But as the day wore on she found herself restless and extremely uneasy. She was unable to enjoy the company of the other guests or even to read. Nothing could allay the nameless fears which her encounter with the nun had caused.

The hunters failed to return at the expected time that evening and not until dusk was fast settling in among the trees was the thud of horses' hooves heard. Nina and Lucia arrived first to meet the hunters. They both noticed that one of the horses was riderless but when the animal came up they were shocked to see that it carried a limp burden upon its back. It was the horse which belonged to Raoul and the animal carried the lifeless body of his master. Raoul had been shot and killed by a friend in a hunting accident.

The story of Nina's experience and her fiancé's tragic death was recorded in a family diary and found many years later in an old desk after the De Saurin home had been sold. Even when the huge house became the Court Inn strange stories were told about the place. One of them concerns a school teacher named Lula Tedder.

After her mother had called to tell her that her

father was critically ill, Miss Tedder left Savannah, Georgia to drive to her home in North Carolina. It was a rainy, foggy day to drive and the coming of darkness made her decide to spend the night at Camden, South Carolina. She remembered the huge old Inn there where she had stayed many years before with her parents.

The Court Inn, that was the name of it. Now, where had the man at the filling station said it would be? Mill and Laurens Streets, that was the address. And there it stood, shrouded in fog and rain. The big square white building with its high steps leading up to the wide veranda was just as she remembered it.

The rain fell in torrents blown by occasional wild gusts which wrenched and tore at the trees. But from within the Inn lights glowed dimly and she could not recall when she had felt so grateful for shelter of any kind.

Lula did not wonder at the fact that the lobby was empty as she walked across the dark red carpet with its old fashioned floral design. However, her eye was caught by a movement at the far rear of the lobby and she was just in time to catch a glimpse of the graceful figure of a young Catholic nun disappearing through a door. Faintly curious she glanced down at the ledger which served as a register and saw three or four other names, but none with the title Sister before it.

A gray-haired bellboy who must have been as ancient as the Inn itself showed her to a large, comfortable room and she decided to ask him if there were any sisters staying at the Inn that night. Tired as she was she felt a vague loneliness and thought a nun might prove good company.

"No, mam. We got no nuns around here," said the old fellow shaking his head vehemently.

"Now, just let me light that fire for you. The way that wind's a blowin' and a wailin' out there 'mongst them trees, we're goin' to have hurricane weather for sure, and you'll be mighty glad to have that fire."

Lula agreed and for awhile was considerably cheered by the orange flames licking hungrily at the resin rich logs of yellow pine. But the wood burned quickly and as the flames sank lower, the shadows in the corners of the room deepened. She became conscious of an acrid, musty odor and the damp chill of the night air began to seep in around her. Although she resolutely tried to ignore it, Lula was having some very peculiar sensations. No matter how hard she tried not to watch the shadows in the corners of the room, particularly the corner near the front window, her eyes kept coming back to it. As the fire grew lower the shadows seemed to leap even more frenetically. She convinced herself that the mirror over the large oak dresser was reflecting some of the flames, distorting them and causing the strange-looking shadows. So, feeling more like herself, she folded her clothes on a chair and went to bed. Lula was almost asleep when she became aware of a soft, rustling sound coming from the corner near the front window. She started up quickly and over in the corner saw the shadowy figure of a young woman.

"Who is there? Tell me who you are," Lula cried out. The woman wore gray garments and they were the habit of a nun. Most disconcerting was the way they seemed to float in the air around her. She passed Lula's bed and as she reached the bedroom door, it swung silently open before her.

Lula remembered the nun she had seen early that evening when she had registered. Why had she appeared in her room and why had the old porter lied? She threw on her robe determined to follow and

103

force this strange visitor to speak to her. The nun moved gracefully down the hall and Lula followed calling "Sister, wait and let me speak to you, please." But the gray-clad nun neither paused nor turned her head to acknowledge that she had heard. She reached the end of the hall and with a swirl of her garments, the nun turned suddenly around and looked Lula full in the face. She was astonishingly beautiful but the dark eyes were full of anguish. Her lips parted as if she were trying to tell Lula something and she seemed to be making a sign with her hands and gesturing toward her left.

At that moment Lula heard the sound of a door open down the hall behind her and voices. She turned at the interruption and when she looked back, the gray lady was gone. Bitterly disappointed she searched the stairwell at the end of the hall and even knocked on the doors of several nearby rooms. One door came open and she saw that at this end of the hall the rooms were not furnished or in use. The young teacher was close to panic but she managed to get back to her room where for the first time in her life Lula Tedder fainted.

When she awoke she could see the gray light of dawn at the edges of the drapes and it was the most glorious sight she had ever seen. The rain had stopped, the night had fled, the corners of the room were no longer dark—nor was there anywhere a shadowy form with misty gray robes floating around her! Lula dressed rapidly and stopped at the desk to pay her bill. The clerk ran his finger down the list of guests on the ledger.

"Jenkins, Thomas, Tedder—why, that's the name of a young man who married into the De Saurin family. This Inn used to be their home, you know."

"No, I didn't, said Lula who felt impatient but managed to smile politely. She paid for her room and the man made no further comment.

She had not driven many miles when the rain began again. Opaque sheets of water struck her windshield with such force she could barely see. Finally, she rolled down the steamy window to decide where she was and whether she was still on the right road. Ahead of her the road forked and she was about to bear right when suddenly the nun's gesture and frantic efforts to tell her something crossed her mind. Had she been pointing left? Lula thought she had and without being sure why or which was the route to take, she bore left.

By mid-afternoon she had reached her home in Asheville and the small Victorian house with its green shutters was a welcome sight. As she opened the front door and walked into the hall, her mother threw her arms around her.

"Lula, I've been so worried about you. Did you know that the bridge on the old road was out?"

"No, I didn't."

"Well, it has been out since the storm yesterday and if I could have phoned you, I would have but I didn't know where you would stay. I was so afraid that you would be in a hurry and try to take the short cut at the fork."

"The short cut at the fork where the roads branch off? You know, I had almost forgotten that spot where either road brings me out at the same place. The one on the left winds about a bit more, but for some reason I took it."

"Well, they would not have brought you out at the same place today," said her mother, and she was right.

There are old residents of Camden who say the

ethereal gray lady walks on starless nights across the barriers of time to haunt the living. But always with compassion. And, if you should meet her you will know there is danger ahead. You will also know that you had a distant relative who once lived in France, a beautiful young nun named Eloise De Saurin.

The Ghost Ship

The doomed colonists saw it and so did the Indians

A lone figure stooped down at the water's edge silhouetted against the sky. It was a timeless scene that might easily have occurred a thousand or so years ago. In the late afternoon light the almost naked form of a man could be seen moving along the shoreline and gathering small shellfish. He was one of North Carolina's Hatteras Indians.

Straightening up suddenly the man gazed out to sea. Motionless and intent he watched the edge of the horizon where a small dark speck was visible. The speck grew larger and larger until the outline was the size of a toy boat, but gradually and unmistakably it became an impressive ship. Its sails stretched full and taut before the gusty autumn wind. With astonishment he saw the vessel head toward Roanoke Inlet.

He turned toward the woods cupping his hands around his mouth and then began beckoning urgently. Other Indians ran out on the beach to join him watching the big three-masted sailing ship go into the inlet. Some began to jump up and down, practically doubling up in their excitement and joy. Well aware of how shallow the inlet was, they knew the ship was certain to wreck. For hadn't many wrecked like this before? For over a hundred years vessels had been going to the bottom in inlets like this one along the Outer Banks and joyful Indians had been salvaging all sorts of unfamiliar but exciting riches including  the nails that they prized so highly.

But this time the most astounding thing happened. With the wind behind it and the triangular flags atop each mast fluttering, this miraculous ship sailed right through the treacherous, shallow water with never a pause. Then it turned and proceeded safely on toward Roanoke Island. The Indians shielded their eyes against the rays of the setting sun to watch. It was an incredible sight and the bewildered savages waiting for the ship to run aground in the shallow water saw it become almost transparent as the afternoon sun shone through it until it faded away, disappearing before their very eyes!

Full of awe and fear they raced toward the undergrowth at the edge of the forest near the shore. A council meeting was held which lasted until the sun rose again. The wise men of the tribe offered many explanations concerning the appearance of the wondrous ship and what it meant.

Surprisingly close to the council meeting dawn was breaking upon a group of men of a very different sort, led by a highly educated, keenly observant Englishman. It was 1703 and John Lawson with a handful of companions was exploring the northern portion of coastal North Carolina, that area which later was called the Outer Banks. Lawson and his men traveled by boat along the rivers and late one fall afternoon two Indians in a canoe paddled out to their boat. One threw beads in Lawson's boat as a sign of love and friendship. Since the explorers were tired he consented to the Indians pleas to go ashore with them.

As soon as they landed they were joined by other Indians of the same tribe bringing a large store of fresh fish, mullet, shad and many other sorts, which they shared with the hungry travelers. Lawson and his men were much impressed by the friendliness and generosity of these tall, well-built Indians with their surprising gray eyes. No other Indians they had met possessed eyes of this color. Normally, their eyes were dark brown, sometimes verging on black.

After the bountiful meal was eaten under the large laurel and bay trees, it was plain the Indians were eager to tell the Englishmen something they considered of the utmost importance. The chief man among them, he who had thrown the beads into their boat, stepped forward and began speaking to Lawson. He gestured often toward the sea and spoke in such an excited manner that his story would have been difficult to follow if Lawson had not learned the language of a number of Indian tribes while roaming the

Early morning light reveals remains of wooden schooner buried in the sand near Nags Head

coastal Carolinas.

As he waved a bronzed arm in the direction of the ocean the other tribesmen stood silently by occasionally nodding vehement assent. Lawson's comrades could catch the word for "by ship," "under full sail" and "talk in a book" which was the Indian way of describing a man who could read.

Lawson's eyes shone with excitement and his men

could scarcely wait for the Indian to finish so that they might learn what he said. None of the Indians added to his story, it being their custom to listen respectfully to a speaker and not interrupt one another. When he had completed the story to his satisfaction, the Indian fell silent and looked at Lawson with unusual warmth and expectancy.

John Lawson responded with the word for brother

at the same time gesturing in a friendly fashion to assure the Indian of his feeling of kinship.

Now it was the Englishmen's turn to hear the story.

"This is not the first time I have heard of this man's experience," said Lawson. "It has been told me by many an Indian wise man when I have been in these parts of Carolina. This man says that many times their tribesmen have seen a ship they were certain was an English sailing vessel come over the horizon and sail quite close to land. It has happened during the day as well as on moonlit nights. Someone among them would look out to sea and there would be an imposing ship under full sail. Quite often it would sail along for a considerable time so that others would gather and watch the ship in amazement as it glided through the water.

"But each time they attempted to paddle out to it in their canoes, it would disappear, filling them with fear and awe. He believes this ship is the one which brought the first colonists to this Island and the Indians call it Sir Walter Raleigh's ship." Lawson stopped to admonish some of the men who were smiling.

"The truth of this has been affirmed to me by men of the best credit in the country." These men say that "several of their ancestors were white people and could talk in a book (read as white men did), the truth of which is confirmed by gray eyes being found frequently amongst these Indians and no others."

Lawson went on to recall to his men the story of the ill-fated colony which John White left in the summer of 1587 in order to bring back badly needed supplies from England. Unfortunately, upon his arrival in England in November, he found his country at war with Spain. Every ship was being commandeered for the struggle and although he begged to be allowed to return to the colony with the supplies they desperately needed, he was refused permission. Meanwhile the colonists suffered and waited watching day and night for the ship's return. In the spring, White optimistically fitted out a small fleet to leave for Roanoke Island. But the Queen of England seized the ships before they could sail. Winning the war with Spain came first.

Those of the colonists who had been able to survive the winter were probably still hopeful. One can imagine them watching the horizon anxiously day after day expecting the arrival of the vessel which would bring the long-awaited clothes, food, medicine and ammunition to relieve their suffering. What rejoicing there would be. As they huddled cold and half-starved along the windswept shores of the island, perhaps they began to have hallucinations. Is it possible their eyes began to supply the ship they wanted so badly to see sailing along that vast, empty, gray-blue horizon of the 1500's?

Some died from sickness, others hunger and, no doubt, they felt more and more abandoned and alone. Their Indian companions who had helped them survive the winter, probably began to watch with them scanning the horizon for the ship the white men talked of constantly, lived for and were so certain would come.

Tragically enough, and despite all his determination, for after all, he had left his daughter and granddaughter on the island, it was not until August of 1590 that John White was able to return. He set sail on the *Hopewell*, one of three ships sent to raid Spanish vessels off the coast of Cuba and capture whatever cargo or treasure they could. Then they were to sail northward up the coast and aid the colonists.

At daybreak on August 18, 1590 White and several sailors got into a small boat and paddled through rough seas to shore. They walked through the woods and rounded North West Point to the place he had left the colonists three years before. White stumbled in his excitement as he climbed the dunes of sand.

At the stop of a forested dune White found a tree on which without any Maltese cross as a sign of distress, had been carved the letters 'CRO.' Bewildered, he walked down to where the settlement had been. There was the high wooden palisade around an enclosure. But the little houses inside were gone. Every building had been taken down. Scattered here and there were some iron bars and pigs of lead, some shot and four cannon. On a post at the right-hand side of the entrance he discovered the word 'CROATOAN.' White thought that this probably meant they had gone inland with Manteo and his friends to Croatoan Island and filled with excitement he wanted to go on southward to the island to look for them.

By now a storm was blowing up. The seas were so rough the men were unable even to load fresh water, the *Hopewell* nearly ran aground and the anchor rope broke so that she had lost one of her two anchors. The weather was becoming more and more treacherous so that with water and food short and only one anchor left they decided it was too dangerous to continue the search.

Completing his story about the ghost ship the Indians told of seeing and the return of White to look for the colonists, John Lawson stared thoughtfully out to sea. It was over one hundred years ago since Captain White had left the doomed colonists on Roanoke Island. Was there really such a thing as a ghost ship? And, if it did exist was it as one Indian wise man had said "an omen" to all the Indians living along the coast that they were in danger from the white man, and that the appearance of the phantom vessel was a forewarning? No one knows.

Reports which are sometimes still heard of a phantom ship sailing over the water through inlets where no real ship could ever go remain as much a mystery today as the fate of the colonists themselves.

Life boat washed up on shore of Hatteras Island

Railroad Bill

For many years this Alabama bandit eluded the law and some still see his ghost near the railroad tracks.

THE BLACK ROBINHOOD
"Railroad Bill mighty bad man,
Shoot dem lights out de brakeman's han'."

There were no screens at the windows of the little unpainted ramshackly house near the railroad tracks. But the old lady was used to that. When the sun went down the night's chill began to settle in she went to each window and hooked the wooden shutter. The old lady fastened them not only to keep out the cold night air but to keep out whatever else might be lurking in the darkness whether man, beast or spirit.

She banked the fire so she would have hot coals in the morning, although she didn't need them to start up the wood in the old wood stove for she had nothing to heat on it, no food and no money to buy food with. Since she had become too old and too crippled by arthritis to work, she had gotten a small check from the welfare but toward the last of the month there never seemed to be enough left even for food. This morning she had fried and eaten a small piece of fatback, all that was left.

She was glad to crawl under the worn quilt on the iron bed and go to sleep for that was the best way not to think about being hungry. Before long, however, she heard a shot ring out and it came from close by. A train's whistle began to emit desperate "toot, toot, toots" and then she could hear men's voices calling out and lots of shouting.

"Don't never hunt trouble," she lay there thinking and not moving. "Bad enuf to be hongry, don' have to go runnin' out to see what everythin's all about and git put in de jail, too. Dat's what happens when po' folks gits in trouble."

About that time Aunt Elly felt the house shake. It

sounded like somebody had come running and taken one big jump, landing right on her back porch. She plumb forgot the misery in her bones and was out of bed and at the back door before you could say spit. Next came a rattling and a clatter on the floor of her porch. She opened the door just in time to see a tall black man standing out there with a big grin stretched across his face, and then he was gone, a straight, broad shouldered figure running across he yard and into the pine woods.

Scattered all over her porch were cans of food and vegetables.

"God bless Railroad Bill," she said looking toward the woods and then as fast as she could she gathered every can and had them in the house and under her bed. This done Aunt Elly crawled back under the quilt. She did not have long to wait.

Soon there was a bounding on her cabin door, It shook the shack from the roof to the floor. Aunt Elly got up and opened the door. There stood the sheriff and a few men more. He asked Aunt Elly if she'd seen Railroad Bill, that he'd robbed a train and would shoot to kill. The old lady made like she was scared to death, said "Oh, mistuh sheriff, keep dat man way from heah. He mighty bad fellah an I hope he don' come neah."

The sheriff said, "Don't you worry, Aunt Elly. We'll get him this time shore. We brung along some bloodhounds. He won't bother folks no more." He turned around and stepped

The railroad telegraph sent word the freight train had been robbed

down from the porch saying, "Tell me, boys, did we bring three hounds or four? Seemed to me we took just three and now I see one more."

But no one paid it any mind and through the woods they went. The dogs were snuffin' on the ground like they had got the scent. But they came right out on the other side with no Railroad Bill in sight, and the sheriff saw the fourth hound dog had vanished in the night. The hair rose on the sheriff's neck and he turned to a friend and said, "That was no bloodhound that ran with the pack, that was Railroad Bill, instead. He's led us a merry chase tonight and he's laughin' in his bed."

For many years this Alabama bandit eluded the law. A black Robin Hood, Railroad Bill robbed freight trains along the Louisville and Nashville Railroad, distributing his loot among the poor. Some say the police finally caught him. Others say his ghost still haunts the pine woods near the tracks, and when some poor old lady finds food outside her door she is more than apt to look each way for the law and then whisper under her breath "God bless Railroad Bill!"

Near this lonely depot in Alabama, Railroad Bill's ghost has been seen walking along the tracks

The Haunted Car

They did not even want to ride in this car for something very strange had happened in it.

Most people are happy to own a new car, but recently a minister and his wife who live in Mississippi wished they did not have one. They wanted very badly to get rid of it. In fact they would even have been glad to have their old car back. It was not that this car did not run perfectly, for it did. But they did not even want to ride in it for something very strange happened when they were in this car and Bill Jamison and his wife were afraid.

It was a brand new shiny gold color four door sedan, a gift from the church Reverend Jamison had served for the past three years. After his secondhand automobile which had the temperament of a donkey about starting, along with a host of other equally endearing qualities, left him stranded half-way to a wedding he was to perform one Saturday, his congregation's natural generosity got the better of them and they decided to given Mr. Jamison a new car.

His wife, Charlene, could sit in it without the

springs jabbing her, the children could roll down the windows without the young minister having to get out and guide the glass back up with his hand if it rained, and the Jamisons began to feel for the first time that having a car was not a series of problems. All went well for the first two weeks.

It was on a Sunday night that Bill and Charlene Jamison decided they would drive to Memphis to see some friends. They were late getting off since Bill had attended a meeting at the church first and both were tired. The Jamisons were driving along from Tupelo to Memphis when suddenly a woman's voice spoke up from the back seat.

"I hope you don't mind my riding with you?" she said, and the minister and his wife turned around to find a little old lady leaning forward with an anxious expression on her face.

Deciding that she must have gotten into the car when they had stopped for gas before leaving Tupelo, Mrs. Jamison assured her they were glad to have her.

"Where can we take you?" asked Jamison.

"You are both very kind," replied the old lady. "I have been sick for several weeks and I'm trying to get to the home of my daughter who lives in Memphis."

"Why, that's no trouble for us at all," said Charlene Jamison. "That's where we happen to be going tonight. You just tell us where we can drop you off."

The little old lady seemed pathetically appreciative and gave them the street address of her daughter's home in Memphis. After that their passenger did not seem particularly inclined to talk and finding herself more tired than she realized, Charlene Jamison fell asleep.

Her husband was intent on his own thoughts and the road so he did not try to make conversation. They drove for some time in silence and it was not until he stopped at a light on the outskirts of Memphis that Charlene awoke. Feeling they had ignored the old lady, she turned around to speak to her. but, to her amazement, the back seat was empty!

Could she have fallen out of the car without their

knowing it? The young couple were shocked and frightened. Something dreadful must have happened to their passenger. They could not imagine how she had left the car without their knowing it. Bill Jamison turned around and drove a number of miles along the road, slowing at country crossroads where he had stopped or paused for caution lights, and the pair strained their eyes looking through the darkness expecting to see the body of the old lady lying beside the road. But they saw no sign of her.

Becoming discouraged, they decided the only thing to do was to turn back to Memphis and find the home of the old lady's daughter. They located the street and the house number she had given them and rang the bell. An attractive young housewife in her early thirties opened the door.

The Jamisons began to tell about finding her mother on the back seat of the car and their distress over her disappearance. As they told her about the old lady's asking them to bring her to this address, tears came to the young woman's eyes.

"My mother has been dead for six months," she said. "This is the third time this has happened and she has appeared to one couple several times."

It was just a few weeks later that the Jamisons decided to visit an auto dealer in Jackson, Mississippi. The salesman was puzzled.

"Now, which car is it out there you said was yours?"

"The gold colored sedan."

"And that's the one you want to trade for another car?"

"Yes," replied the minister patiently.

"Sorry, sir, I wasn't trying to be rude. But it's not often somebody brings a car in that looks like new and says they want to trade it. Been having any motor trouble?'"

"No, the motor's in good condition. I just want to trade cars. There's a car over there," and he pointed to a brand new gold colored sedan.

"Yes, sir, but that's the same model you're driving."

"I know that. Do you mind telling me how much I can trade for?"

The young salesman went out and looked at the mileage on the minister's car. Then he did some figuring in his office.

"I'm sorry, but it's going to come to $750.00. You know your car does have some mileage on it and we can't sell it for new."

"I understand that. Can we finance the difference?"

The salesman figured out what the monthly payments would be and the minister and his wife signed the necessary papers.

After they were through he said, "If you don't mind, sir, I sure would like to know why you wanted to trade that car."

"Mind? No, not a bit. That car is haunted and I don't ever want to see it again!"

With that Bill and Charlene Jamison drove off in the car they had just purchased leaving the salesman staring after them, if anything more bewildered them ever. He gazed over at the car they had left behind them. Was that his imagination or had someone gotten into the car? It looked almost like the profile of a little old lady sitting on the back seat. He shook his head in disbelief and walked a little closer, but when he could see in the rear side window better, there was no one there at all.

He glanced around to be sure none of the other salesmen had seen his odd behaviour. Better sell that car before we're all crazy around here, he thought, and he walked toward a couple who had just come into the salesroom.

Volume Two

GHOSTS of the SOUTHERN MOUNTAINS and APPALACHIA

CONTENTS

Contents

GHOSTS of the SOUTHERN MOUNTAINS and APPALACHIA

Night of the Hunt

Hendersonville, North Carolina

In the North Carolina mountains south of Asheville and nearer Hendersonville, it was a good hunting night. You might even go so far as to say, it was the best of all nights and the worst of all nights for after it, neither dog nor hunters would ever be the same again. It is too bad, because this particular dog was his owner's pride and joy.

It was the time of year when it began to get dark early but wasn't too cold, and the sky was full of shifting clouds. Wheeler and his friend, Tom McDuffy, were riding along in Wheeler's old blue Ford pick-up along Highway 25 south of Hendersonville. String Bean, a black and tan coon dog, was in the back, and to hear Jim Wheeler tell it, no dog ever lived that was this one's equal. He began to explain to his inexperienced friend how the hunt goes.

1

"Coons like dark nights and they tree better on nights like this instead of just heading for a hole in the ground," explained Jim who had been trying to talk his friend into going with him for a long time.

"Tom, it gets into your blood and in the fall when the darkness begins to come early, you think about walking through the leaves, seeing your breath make smoke curls in the night air and watching the sky hoping the moon's not going to come out and light up the whole woods."

"What are we trying to do, though?"

"Well, the purpose of coon hunting is to tree the coon."

"Yes, I know that but to me String Bean's no different from other dogs, You act like he's human."

"What are you talking about. String Bean's won more coon hunt trophies than any dog in North or South Carolina either. I did hear onetime there was a dog over in Tennessee that had won just as many; but that may have been String Bean's grand-daddy. Tennessee's where all the great coon dogs come from, though."

"What makes one of these 'great coon dogs' you're talkin' about?"

"Well, I'll tell you. They got to be able to run all night and they got to have a nose that can tell the trail of a coon from a possum."

"What else?"

"Now, take String Bean, when he's after a coon nothing in heaven or earth's goin' to distract him. A deer could start 'buck dancing' right in front of him and he'd pass on by. But the main thing about a

good dog is his bark. As soon as String Bean picks up the scent he'll bark to let me know and then, as he chases the coon, he'll bark every couple of minutes to let me know which direction he's running in. That's his trailin' bark."

"What kind of bark does that one sound like?"

"Well, it's not his regular bark. You just get so you know it. Then when he's got the raccoon treed he'll give out a series of continuous barks. String Bean can just about talk to me," said Jim proudly.

By this time the two men had reached a side road north of Flat Rock where they turned off. They bounced down the rutted dirt road, skirting pot holes, for several miles on the way to their favorite hunting spot. The woods they were headed for was just the other side of the old Culpepper place not far from Pisgah Forest. When the pick-up rolled to a stop, Jim let String Bean out of the back of the truck and started talking to him.

"You're gonna have a good time tonight, String Bean. The weather's just right for us and that coon." Only the silhouettes of the bare tree branches could be seen against the dark sky. Gnarled limbs of oak trees gestured awkwardly overhead, a few beeches still wore some of their bright brown leaves and the big tulip poplars stood like white skeletons in the night. The hunters adjusted and lighted their carbide lamps fixing them to their caps. String Bean watched and waited. He knew the night was his and there would be coons out there just for him.

At last they were ready to take the dog off his leash. With a "Go get 'um!" from Jim, String Bean was off. For a few seconds his paws could be heard hitting the carpet of old leaves on the ground as he circled about in the woods, then the rustling sounds faded and the men were left in the darkness and quiet of the Carolina woods. They were far enough away from Hendersonville so that there was no reflection of lights in the sky nor a sound to be heard from the distant highway. It was like being the last two men alive.

The carbide lamps made them look almost like coal miners in some dark, deep tunnel rather than hunters. Actually, it was past the season when you could shoot raccoons and neither man carried a gun. They were there to hear the dog run, to get away from their wives for an evening and for something else they couldn't have put into words if they tried. Perhaps, it was to experience that awesome feeling of being remote from civilization, out there alone in the woods on this ink-black night.

Whatever each man's thoughts were, they were interrupted by a bark. String Bean's voice floated back saying he had found the trail of a coon. Jim and Tom stood leaning against the truck. Now they would wait until the dog's bark indicated he had the coon treed. When it came they would make their way to him while String Bean would give out almost continuous barks to keep the coon in the uppermost branches and the hunters on course to the tree.

Another trailing bark came a minute later from beyond the far side of the hill, and then another but Wheeler heard nothing that sounded like the bark of a dog who has the coon treed. After the two barks a long silence followed. "That's not like String Bean to go all this time without barking," said Jim after they had waited about ten minutes. Tom didn't reply but he felt a chill as if the night had suddenly turned cold, which it hadn't. They walked around the truck restlessly, the beams from the carbide lamps on their caps darting back and forth, as they turned their heads this way and that, hoping to hear something from out there in the darkness.

"You've 'muched' over that dog so, I'd like to know where he is now," said Tom. Jim didn't reply to the jibe. This hadn't happened before and he waited for his dog's voice to tell him which way to go.

Then it came but it was no trailing bark. He had never heard String Bean sound that way for this was a long, frightened, wailing bark as if the animal had run into something he could not ken, something far beyond the edge of his knowledge. Without saying a word the men started off through the darkness in the direction of the last unearthly yelp, their pale beams of light painting the tree branches white wherever they swept across them.

They got their bearings as they crested the hill. Ahead of them lay a little 'basement' of blackness where the ruins of the old Culpepper place stood, surrounded by a tangle of vines. Betwixt them and the house lay a pond and beyond it they now saw a dim pinpoint of light. They were making their way carefully around the pond toward the house and were just at the water's edge, when they heard it for the first time. It was a sound that floated and hung suspended in the darkness. Melodic, lingering it seemed to wrap each note around them leaving a plaintive trail in the air.

"Nobody's lived in that house in over fifty years," said Jim.

"Well, somebody is in there now," said Tom trying to tell himself that he wasn't really hearing anything out of the ordinary. For the first time since they had started out, they heard a whimper and it came from the direction of the house.

It was String Bean and he was on the front porch, his nose pointing to the door. Now and then, he would whimper again. The two men crept up closer, the candlelight from one of the windows their guide.

"Who could be living in this old wreck of a place?" Tom seemed to think he had to whisper.

"I don't rightly know."

"Well, I hope it ain't hants."

"I'm goin' to knock," said Jim and knock he did, but nobody opened the door. For a few seconds there was silence and then inside the house a fiddle struck up an old tune that was somewhere in Jim's memory but too far back for him to get a hold on.

"I hear music and dancing."

"Must be having a party in there and just can't hear us," said Tom.

He struck the door several hard licks with his fist. But the fiddling went on unabated and no one came to the door. Suddenly they heard thunder and a gust of wind fingered the sprigs of the shrubs against the house.

"Let's go. It's goin' to set to rainin'."

"No it's not. I want to see in the window," said Jim. They stopped in front of a high window with an old brick chimney beside it.

"Lift me up some, Tom. I got to see those people in there. Tom made a stirrup of his hands and the other man pulled himself up enough to look in. The scene before him would stay with Jim Wheeler the rest of his life. A cold chill went through him. As Wheeler watched he began to tremble.

"Jim. You're shakin' so I can't hardly hold you up. What's the matter?" Jim Wheeler didn't answer but just kept staring in the window. Tom had now managed to pull himself up enough to see in, too. Both men were transfixed by the macabre scene before them. A bride and groom were dancing together. When the set ended the girl, dressed in a yellowed wedding dress, started toward the table with the candle on it.

She's going to put it out thought Jim but as he watched her reach the table, he was dumbfounded to see her pass right through it! The train of her wedding dress brushed across the candle flame and it never even flickered! Wheeler's heart turned a cartwheel but he clung to the sill with one foot on the chimney and the other lodged in a place where a board was off. Then he saw them start up again swirling and tromping, looking at each other as though hypnotized and not getting a mite out of step as they moved rhythmically to the sound of fiddle and banjo.

How long the two hunters continued to watch, neither knew. Perhaps it was minutes or perhaps just seconds when suddenly the candle within was extinguished and all was dark and quiet. Both men dropped to the ground. Tom stepped on a brick, fell, picked himself up and then he and Jim were running a foot race to see which could leave the fastest. Fortunately, Wheeler thought to stop and call String Bean and the dog was soon beside them, glad to be in human company again. Branches slapped against their faces as they ran and the briars were like sharp claws tearing at their clothes some piercing the flesh beneath. It didn't matter. In their haste, they ran wide of the truck and had to stop and get their bearings before they finally found it.

Wheeler didn't take String Bean out again that winter and the next season he found another hunting place miles north of Hendersonville. But there was a hard to define difference in both man and dog. Jim noticed that it was a long time before his pleasure in the hunt returned. As for String Bean, it was months before his bark took on its old, confident tone and sometimes Wheeler thought it would never again sound the way it once had. The dog had felt whatever was happening there as surely as the men had seen it. It wasn't menacing, it just wasn't part of this world, something that animals are often aware of even before people.

The story of the dancing bride has been told by the old people of the area for many years and Jim and Tom were not the first to hear the music and see the ghostly pair celebrate their vows. Finally, a researcher discovered that in the late 1890s an elaborate wedding had taken place there but the bride, sticken with scarlet fever, had died a few weeks later.

Some say the spirits of the bride and groom are this young couple continuing to return almost a century later to celebrate their wedding day. Not

long ago a man near Flat Rock told the story of what
he had seen.

"The fiddler's were just fiddlin' away and when
a voice sang out 'Swing your partner,' you've never
seen a girl float through the air like that one did
when the groom swung out his bride. Even now, it
gives me cold chills all the way down my spine just to
think about it." The group listening to him were
silent.

Then, an eighteen year old boy spoke up, "I'm
ready to go out there tonight if somebody will go
with me." But no one volunteered or even looked
his way and the story teller went on talking medita-
tively.

"It was about five years ago late at night when I
passed that way. Some says in my grand-daddy's
day there used to be young 'uns all over the place,
foreigners comin' from way off and lots of play parties. A fine house stood there 'oncet'. I'm a 'goin'
back some day 'cause I want to see that bride and
groom dancing together one more time before I
die, but not right yet."

Return of the Bell Witch

Adams, Tennessee

"I think she is back," says Carney Bell, descendant of the man whose death the Bell Witch is said to have caused. Mr. Bell, one of the owners of Austin and Bell Funeral Home at Springfield, Tennessee has had experiences that prove to him that the most famous witch of the nineteenth century is here and up to her old tricks.

"Not long before my mother died, she was frightened and called me to come over and check the house. She had heard a loud series of crashes and stayed in her bedroom calling me from the upstairs phone. Mother lived about five doors from our home. When I arrived I checked every door—there are seven outside doors—and every one of

12

them was locked. But when we went in the pantry her best glassware had fallen from the shelves and lay all over the floor. The shelves ranged from four to six feet from the floor and yet nothing was broken! If I hadn't seen it for myself I wouldn't have believed it."

How could some malevolent being, who first appeared almost 200 years ago, still roam the area north of Nashville, near Adams, Tennessee today? Yet, that is exactly what seeems to be happening. The account of the Bell Witch is probably the most widely documented story of the supernatural in America, not only because of the marker erected to her by the State of Tennessee Department of Archives and History, but because so many people have had a personal encounter with her.

After causing John Bell's death she announced she would be gone for a century, but that has past. Now, people like W. M. Eden who owns a portion of the original Bell farm, John Bell's descendant, Carney Bell, and numerous others believe the Bell Witch has come back just as she promised to do.

Heaven knows that Kate had every reason to return in the first place. In the opinion of this writer, few apparitions come back to haunt any of us for revenge. They simply happen to be there—at the same place we are at the same moment in time. But that does not include this particular spirit who some say suffered at the hands of one man. She returned for revenge.

"I believe in Kate," says W. M. Eden. He is a white-haired man, dressed in a blue plaid shirt and overalls. "She's never hurt me but there have been nights when I have had to really fight just to keep the covers on my bed; and I've heard footsteps as near to me as that bedroom door." But let us go back many years and to another state where the story first began.

In the late 1770s a hard-working young man named John Bell lived alone in his cabin in Halifax County, North Carolina. He was not planning to remain alone, however, for he was engaged to a lady who owned a large tract of farm land. Her name was Kate Batts, a prominent name belonging to one of the first settlers of eastern North Carolina. After her husband's death, John Bell had stopped at her farmhouse now and then to help her with the settling of the estate. Less than a year after she had donned the black widow's attire, which only accentuated her white skin and cloud of waist length black hair, the pair announced their engagement.

But scarcely were they engaged when John began to learn that the widow had a vile temper and a sharp tongue. He searched for ways to break off with Kate but she would not listen. The farm was more than she could handle alone and she was determined that John Bell would become her husband and farm it. The unfortunate man, who had been blind enough to think this woman capable of any love or kindness, could only imagine what it would be like to live with her. He was in torment.

On a winter afternoon they had been out riding over Kate's farm and discovered that a building of hers needed repairing. John's tools were at his cabin and when they rode over there to get them, the widow was thirsty. As she drew water from the

3C　38

BELL WITCH

To the north was the farm of John Bell, an early, prominent settler from North Carolina. According to legend, his family was harried during the early 19th century by the famous Bell Witch. She kept the household in turmoil, assaulted Bell, and drove off Betsy Bell's suitor. Even Andrew Jackson who came to investigate, retreated to Nashville after his coach wheels stopped mysteriously. Many visitors to the house saw the furniture crash about them and heard her shriek, sing, and curse.

TENNESSEE　HISTORICAL　COMMISSION

This is the only historic sign known that commemorates a witch! Recent accounts indicate that the witch is back after her absence of a century.

well, a freak accident occurred and she was struck in the forehead by the heavy bucket. She gave a little cry and collapsed. John bathed her face but, unable to revive her, began to fear she was dead.

His next thought was that others would believe he was to blame. Carrying the limp form down to his root cellar beneath the house, he left her there. Unlike some cellars of this sort, it could be locked from within the house by means of a trap door.

That night and all the next day everything was quiet. Terrified over his predicament, he knew he must soon find a place to bury her. Then, as he prepared for bed, he heard a sound near his hearth and just above the root cellar. It was a dragging sound followed by moans. In the middle of the night he was still awake; and it must have been two in the morning when he heard his name called.

"John, help me. Please help me." He tried to believe he had heard nothing. But the sounds went on. "I'm so hungry. Water . . . please." And so it went for the rest of the night. His dog began sniffing the crack around the trap door and with a kick, John sent the dog hurtling out of the cabin. He examined all the possibilities. If he brought her up, she would cause a scandal because of his leaving her down there so long. The only way to keep her from doing that would be to go ahead and marry her and that was unthinkable. He knew she would never let him go, and her temper was such that she would have her own way or die in the attempt. Realizing this, he knew what he had to do. He did not open the trap door.

The next morning he was exhausted but he spent the day taking care of his animals and repairing some of his own farm buildings. By late afternoon when he returned the faint cries had ceased and all was quiet. When he cautiously entered the root cellar with a candle late that night, he found she was dead. Loading the body on the sled he used to haul firewood, he pulled it to her house and around back beside her own well. There he left it. An old half-blind crone who sometimes helped Widow Batts with the vegetable garden discovered Kate the next morning.

For several months it was as if a tremendous weight had been lifted from him. He met a kind, understanding young woman named Lucy Williams and soon proposed to her. John and Lucy Bell had not been married long when he decided to sell his farm in North Carolina and start a new life in Tennessee. Buying a thousand acre farm on the banks of the Red River about fifty miles north of Nashville not far from the Kentucky border, he brought his family to settle in Robertson County in 1804. But he was to have only a few peaceful years.

Walking along while plowing one day he looked over to see a monstrous, inky black bird with fiery eyes sitting on a fence post staring at him. He had never seen anything like it before. Even when he walked toward it the bird did not move but sat motionless, glaring fiercely at him. He shouted at it and the creature flew toward him swooping down as if to attack but swerving at the last second with a horrendous fluttering of wings. It passed above him so close that he was overwhelmed by the most dreadful stench as it barely cleared the top of his head. That was the first peculiar event he would later remember.

It is not easy to pin down when the scraping of pear tree branches against the large one and one-half story log house and other normal noises made a transition to sounds of the most eerie nature. According to one of his sons, Richard, he and his three brothers were asleep in an upstairs bedroom and awakened to hear a noise like an enormous rat gnawing on the bedpost. They got up to investigate but as soon as a candle was lit all was quiet and nothing could be seen. The moment the candle was blown out, the noise began again.

This horrible, gnawing sound was soon heard every night and it moved from one room to another in the Bell house. Then came a series of most repulsive noises as if someone were smacking their lips while they ate, alternating with loud gulps that resembled choking or strangling. And if it seemed that there was peace for a few hours, in the midst of the family's relieved slumbers the covers would be jerked off their beds as if snatched by some unseen hand. But worst of all, an invisible presence twisted and jerked the children's hair until they ran screaming in fright.

At first the Bell's said nothing to anyone about these events. Finally, John Bell told his close friend and neighbor Jim Johnson and the Johnsons came over to spend the night. It was to be the most unpleasant night of their lives.

They had no sooner retired than the noises started. It began with loud knocking followed by gnawing, scratching and smacking. The chairs in the Johnsons' bedroom overturned. Bedcovers flew off. The Bell's daughter, Betsy, was slapped across the face by invisible hands and the entire house was soon in pandemonium. The Johnsons could hardly be expected to keep all this to themselves and when word was out about the strange happenings the curious began to arrive from all over Tennessee. Some came to investigate and others to help if they could. About this time another mystifying spectacle occurred. Lights could be seen flitting through the trees in the Bell yard and across the fields of the farm.

Now, the family began to try to talk to whatever it was by asking questions such as how many people are in the room, how many horses are in the yard or whatever could be answered with a number of knocks. The answers were always correct. And then the thing began to talk. Words first came in a harsh, disembodied voice that gradually gained strength and grew more feminine. It was soon apparent that the thing had a passionate hatred for John Bell and whether it first revealed its identity to him or some other member of the family, all soon knew it as, Kate Batts' witch.

When Bell first learned this he went into deep depression. Not that he was the only person who was the object of her attentions, but it was for him that she reserved her most vicious acts and now that she could be understood, her oath to kill him was unmistakable.

But for many it was a most entertaining phenomenon. The question often arose as to whether you can touch a ghost. Visitors to the Bell house were curous about this, and on one occasion Calvin Johnson, who Kate frequently talked with, asked her if he could shake her hand. She was reluctant to do this but finally agreed that she would do so if he

This cave where the witch is said to have made her home is on a portion of the old Bell farm north of Nashville.

would promise not to try to hold or grasp her hand. He stretched out his hand and within seconds something soft lay in it, like the hand of a woman. No one doubted him who was watching his expression when it happened. His brother, Jack, made the same request but Kate refused him saying, "No, I don't trust you. You are a grand rascal, Jack Johnson."

Visitors sometimes found Kate embarrassing as she revealed their darkest secrets, poked fun at them, joined blasphemously in religious discussions and when she raided a nearby still house she would keep everyone up all night with her frightful oaths and drunken singing. Kate performed for a constant stream of visitors and about this time an entire "family" of spirits joined her at the Bell farm. Now, there were five distinct disembodied voices including Kate's. While the other four spirits came and went, Kate stayed with the Bell family and, particularly, with John Bell; but she would never explain why she hated him so.

Two years went by and John Bell began to suffer mysterious attacks in which his tongue would swell and stiffen in his mouth. He would be unable to eat or talk and described the feeling as similar to having a sharp stick wedged crossways in his mouth. Kate would interrupt the concern of his wife and family when he was having these spells by laughing raucously at his suffering. His afflictions grew more frequent and more terrible almost making him an invalid and the witch cursed him viciously all the while.

On the morning of December 19, 1820 his wife was unable to wake him from an unnaturally deep sleep. His son, John, Jr., went to the medicine cupboard but his prescription bottle was missing and in its place was another vial with a dark, smoky liquid. As usual, Kate was among them.

"I've got him this time," she crowed gleefully. "He'll never get up from that bed again," said Kate. And she was right, he never did.

When asked about the vial in the cupboard she replied, "I put it there myself. I gave Old John a big dose of it last night while he was asleep and that fixed him." The family put some of the liquid on a straw and drew it through a cat's mouth sending the animal into an immediate convulsion. John Bell died the next day. Even at his funeral Kate disrupted the solemn ceremony with raucous, drunken singing during the burial service in the family graveyard.

In 1821, the witch surprised everyone by announcing that she was leaving but would return in seven years. Her homecoming in February of 1828 was marked by a return of the knockings, gnawings, and scratchings on the outside walls of the house and the pulling off of covers from the beds. This time, however, the Bell Witch stay was brief. After Mrs. Bell's death the farm was divided, and it was not surprising that no one wanted to live in the old house which was eventually torn down. But this was not to be the end of the Bell Witch. As she left, she swore to return in a hundred years. Recent events indicate her promise is being fulfilled.

In a publication called the "Tennessee Traveler," Don Wick writes of encounters people are having with the Bell Witch in the twentieth century in the cave near the banks of the Red River. They report various phenomena such as the figure of a dark-haired woman floating through the cave passages, the sounds of chains dragging along the stone floor, footsteps and unearthly cries. W. M. Eden who has owned this part of the Bell farm for many years has had his share of personal experiences "with Kate or whatever it is inside that cave."

"On a winter's day a few years ago there was new snow on the ground. I heard someone knocking at my front door and looked through the window. When I saw the outline of a figure I didn't recognize I went to get my shotgun. By the time I returned, the form was walking toward a large tree in the yard but it never came out on the other side, so I went out the back door and around to the tree but found no one. My shoes were making prints in the fresh snow but from the front door to the tree the snow was as smooth and undisturbed as if it had just fallen and there were no footprints at all."

Carney Bell, one of the present day descendants of John and Lucy Bell, has had his own odd experiences in recent years which he attributes to Kate.

"Some things that have happened in the family are almost like a coincidence. For instance when I was watching television one night and a next door neighbor called to tell me there was a program on one of the channels about the Bell Witch, I turned to that channel but could only get wavy lines. After trying two other sets in the house, we gave up. Yet I found that the neighbors on each side of us were viewing it!"

According to Eden, a group of soldiers from Fort Knox, Kentucky came to explore the dark, dank recesses of the cave and one of the soldiers poked fun at the story of Kate. "A few minutes later he was lying on the floor of the cave. He shouted for help saying he could feel something sitting on his chest and squeezing the breath right out of him. I don't think he will forget his sensation in that cave when something grasped him and pinned him to the ground."

Strange, floating lights appear in the fields of the farm owned by W. M. Eden, and many have chased the elusive lights only to have them vanish and reappear a short distance away. In this area around Adams, Tennessee, the Bell Witch is not just a legend—she is a strong presence.

My own visit to the cave was an interesting, if eerie, experience. As we came out into the welcome, fresh night air, Mr. Eden stopped and looked back over his shoulder. There was an air of expectancy about the way he stood there looking back at the cave as if he might see something emerge at any moment.

That night there was no sign of anything in the darkness behind us, but Eden told of the time "I was in the cave with my German shepherd dog, Fritz, when we heard a sound back in the innermost recesses of the cavern as if a heavy object was being dragged noisily along the stone floor. I sat down on a ledge to see what would happen and Fritz sat quietly beside me. The sound grew closer and louder. I knew something was about to round the curve in the wall of the cavern just a few feet away.

"At that point Fritz who weighs at least 75 pounds leaped into my lap! The noise grew louder and whatever it was went right past us while the dog huddled against me and I could feel the animal trembling. After waiting for two or three minutes, we both raced for the entrance. What was it? I think it was Kate." Eden believes that her spirit roams the Adams area day and night.

"I've known for years that cave is a strange place; but it's where Kate lives now. They say she was gone for a hundred years but, I believe she's home for good."

When this story was written the cave could be toured by contacting Mr. W. M. Eden of Adams, Tennessee.

The Shenandoah Stage

New Market, Virginia

Two young Confederate officers sat eating together in the dining room of the Hotel in New Market, Virginia on the evening of May 24, 1862. General Stonewall Jackson, who would become Lee's right arm, had just won his first important battle the day before at Front Royal. Was there any way for the Union to stop him now? Perhaps, and perhaps not.

The officers had seen the man seated at the bar looking at them and decided he must be a Confederate sympathizer. Judging by his lack of a pistol, his imported suit and well manicured hands he could be a writer or a minister visiting in the New Market area, perhaps, en route to Richmond. Fleming raised a gray clad arm gesturing for him to join them and the stranger responded eagerly.

Slim and immaculately groomed, the dark-haired young man sat down introducing himself as John Sharp, and as he spoke there were traces of a British accent. After a few minutes of evaluating him, both officers had decided that he was British and sympathetic to the Southern cause. Lt. Henry Fleming voiced his gratitude for the Enfield rifles that had been getting through the blockade and the gentleman smiled and nodded.

"Why is England so slow to recognize the Confederacy formally?"

"Mr. Fleming, I don't know, but I understand it will not be long before an ambassador will be sent to Richmond."

"Of course England needs our cotton if the textile mills are to keep running," said Lt. MacRae. "Isn't that so?"

"My dear friend, I can assure you that even now, important decisions are being made in England."

"Important decisions have been made here and it's time they did something to recognize us," said Stewart MacRae who was a South Carolinian.

"Columbia is such a beautiful city. I greatly enjoyed my recent stay there," said John Sharp changing the subject. His accent was pleasant to the ears of MacRae whose hopes for an education abroad had been postponed because of the war.

"You have just come from Columbia then?"

"Indeed I have. Is it possible I met your sister at a musical there . . . no, surely not. That would be too much of a coincidence. I think this girl's name was . . ."

"Letitia?"

"Of course. I recall it because this Letitia exemplified everything I had imagined about Southern womanhood."

"I can't believe it. You met my dearest sister. And how was she?"

"She was delightful."

"I don't know when I have had a letter from her but the mail doesn't keep up with General Jackson, you know."

"They say his men worship him now."

"He takes care of them—with General Banks' storehouses of supplies! Jackson manages to see that we get more than our fair share," said Fleming with a smile. Everyone joked about the way Jackson kept capturing the Union General's supplies and they even called Banks, "Jackson's commissary."

"You gentlemen will be resting here in New Market for a week or so, now, won't you?" said Sharp.

Fleming stiffened ever so slightly and the glass of wine on the way to his lips stopped in midair. "Why do you ask, sir?"

"Just an off-hand remark. I imagine the men jolly well need it for they have been on the march a great deal and I would think they must be tired. What do you say, MacRae?"

"Well, sometimes the men say he is 'marching them to death to no good end' but I know the General when he gets started. Winchester is only a few miles up the . . ."

"Hush! Stewart. We don't know what the General's got in his mind. No one does," said Lt. Fleming.

At that moment a courier approached the two Confederate officers and told them they were to join their regiment at once.

"We're marching?" asked MacRae and the courier nodded.

"Where is the good fellow who sat with you gentlemen?" asked one of the bartenders as they paid their bill.

"The Britisher?"

"He isn't a Britisher, he went to Harvard."

"Harvard?"

"Yes. My brother went there and picked up the accent. I knew I'd heard it before and I asked him. He finally admitted it, but said he had always been a Southern sympathizer." Fleming shook his head and grasped MacRae by the arm. "Did you hear that?"

"Certainly. But I know a Southern sympathizer when I meet one." They passed Sharp who was part of a group outside the hotel without noticing him.

The valley stage had just pulled up. The passengers and driver were entering the hotel for the evening meal. The stage was a familiar sight on the road to Winchester thought Sharp; and then an idea came to him as he stood there alone for a moment in the dusk. The thought was at once so practical and opportune that he leaped up into the driver's seat and seized the reins. In the interval since the vehicle had arrived, the street in front of the New Market Hotel had emptied and it seemed there was no one to see his deed. The stage was off to a mud-splattering, clattering start.

When he reached the edge of town, Sharp cracked his whip to urge the horses on. And, so, with this stage rode the fate of General Banks at Winchester and Stonewall Jackson's army on the way to attack.

Back in New Market the two young Confederate officers were saddling their horses in the stable next to the hotel building. There was no reason to hurry because it takes an army of 17,000 men more than a few minutes to get started. They had heard the clatter of the stage as it left and now looked up amazed to see the driver come running into the stable shouting, "Help! Someone has stolen my stage."

They cantered around to the front of the hotel and Fleming saw the man he had talked to at the bar. "Where is our Harvard man?" he called out and the fellow shook his head and replied, "He rushed off without paying his bill!"

"Let's go, Stewart. Spur your horse!"

"What do you mean? We've got a long road ahead of us."

"Our friend in the Hotel has taken off in the valley stage. He was a spy and we gave away Jackson's plan."

"Good Lord! We've got to stop him before he reaches the Union lines and warns Banks," said MacRae. And so, the "great valley chase" started there in the last twilight of May 24th, 1862. Ahead, the stagecoach pulled by four slightly worn horses followed by two young Confederates on fresh mounts. The stage probably had a two mile lead as they left New Market but the officers were Jackson's men and they were more than good "foot cavalry" as they sometimes derisively called themselves, they rode well, too.

By the time they passed the crossroads at Mt. Jackson the lead had narrowed to a half mile. The stagecoach horses were tiring, not used to such a wild pace. At Edinburg at midnight the Confederate officers could see the stage in the moonlight only a few hundred yards in front of them. And at the same time they saw the stage, Sharp saw his two pursuers. They would catch him before he could reach help—unless he used his Navy revolver. He hated to do that. Odd, that it had been MacRae's sister he met, and for one of the few times in his life, he was much taken with a woman. What irony to have to shoot the girl's brother. He cursed to himself. He wished now he had never followed his intuition and asked MacRae her name back at the Hotel.

The smell of rain had been in the air earlier at Mt. Jackson and now it had started. Cool drops tapped his face as the stage swept under the storm. What a spectacle the lightning was! He might not have to do anything, he thought. Most horsemen were afraid of lightning and rightfully so. Of course, it could strike the stage but caught up in the excitement of the chase he laughed aloud for he loved danger. Anyway, would the Devil harm his own? Or, if God was really on the Union side, he was safe either way!

But his pursuers, now only a short distance behind him, were undiscouraged by the sharp cracks of lightning so Sharp turned on the seat and took aim. He knew what he had to do and he would not miss. He could see the dark shapes of the two horsemen and he did not know which was MacRae and which was Fleming in the blackness. And then he had a moment of indecision. He had shared a meal with these two men and liked them both so they were no longer strangers. But what was his alternative? If he stopped he would become their prisoner and very likely be hanged. He would not, could not do that. Sharp had learned marksmanship well and he waited for them to ride even closer before he sighted down the barrel. Then he pulled the trigger.

As he did so a blast engulfed the stage but it came not from the pistol but from the clouds. Lightning struck right on the metal barrel just as the pistol was about to fire engulfing the man and the stage; and thunder came at the same second as it often does when lightning hits close by. The two Confederates reined their horses to a stop, momentarily blinded by the flash; then came thunder crashing around them and rumbling off to the South. Neither man was sure what had happened until they saw the charred outlines of the stage.

They were alone in the darkness with a dead spy who had tried to kill them, their nostrils inhaling the strong smell of horses wet from a mixture of sweat and spring rain, the storm subsiding and Jackson's suprise attack building up somewhere out in the night. They rejoined their regiment and for many reasons the entire episode was one they never really cared to talk about.

On the next day General Stonewall Jackson attacked the Federal line at Winchester and broke it and General Banks' men fled desperately toward the Potomac. His army escaped destruction but it was a panic-stricken retreat, little better than a rout. The people of Winchester looked upon the Confederate troops as saviors giving them an ecstatic welcome almost "demented with joy."

Now Jackson's men knew what they had been marching for and bitterness was replaced by elation over their dazzling triumph. Confidence in him and themselves soared and word of Jackson's feat spread as General Banks' star plummeted. The man who had stolen the stage, John Sharp, was no Britisher but, in reality a second lieutenant in the Union cavalry and the son of a wealthy Boston ship owner. His schooling had been at Harvard and his accent was deceptive. At Banks' request Lt. Sharp had volunteered to spy for the Union and was traveling up and down the valley collecting information on the movements of Stonewall Jackson's men.

A year later, Leland Hawes, a scout for Colonel Moseby, saw what he thought was the old valley stagecoach flying along at top speed, the horse's hoofs scarcely touching the ground. Its driver was glancing behind him as he urged his horses on. Then thunder rolled across the valley and clouds obscured the face of the moon. When they vanished, Hawes looked again but this time he saw nothing and for many years the stage was reported here and there between New Market and Winchester.

Only when the moon is full, only when rain is in the air and only when clouds drift over the face of the moon causing dark shadows is the stage seen again in our day. As it travels along old Highway 11, once called the Valley Pike, its fading red paint is splattered with mud and the driver's face is deadly pale and streaked by smoke. His bony, blackened hands grip the reins tightly as the stagecoach bounces over the ruts and stones of the old road.

But it's those four white horses that take your breath away to watch. In full gallop they strain at the creaking leather harness, manes flowing, hoofs flying. Why the hurry? Where are they going?

The stage is headed to Winchester more than a hundred years late, both driver and team captives of another dimension in time. They are destined to ride forever but never to arrive. How many visions like Sharp and the valley stagecoach are out there for us to encounter one of these nights on some remote mountain road or lonely deserted place? Like debris from this world left in space that will go whirling about forever, are we experiencing something left long ago on our planet from other lives, the eerie debris of the spirit-world?

Chain Gang Man

Decatur, Alabama

It was Sunday morning and he had been sitting on the porch of his Pa's cabin back up in the Alabama hill country strumming his guitar and singing to himself.

> "O hand me down that corpse of clay
> That I may look upon it.
> I might have saved that life,
> If I had done my duty."

The tune was, "Barbara Allen," and a sad one, but for some reason the twenty-year old boy with curly black hair and gentian blue eyes had always liked it. To his surprise he saw a cloud of dust with a black Ford in the midst of it come jouncing along the seldom traveled dead-end road. Two law men got out of the car.

"You Lonnie Stephens?"

"Yeah, I'm Lonnie."

"Then come with us, an' if you come peacable, you won't get hurt."

Lonnie stood up in surprise and they took it for assent, but when they tried to put handcuffs on him he fought hard. It was not until they subdued him that he found out why they were here.

"We know you done killed her and you mought as well make a clean breast 'a it."

"Killed who?"

"Cordelia. Ain't that your girlfriend?"

"Dead? She can't be!"

"It was your gun what shot her. We done identified that and it wan't no trouble 'cause you dropped it in the woods right near her body."

Lonnie lifted both arms to bring the handcuffs down on the head of one of his captors but the other lawman saw his intention and butted him in the side so that he lost his balance and fell to the ground. "He resisted arrest all right," the man who had very nearly worn handcuffs on his head later testified at the trial. "He was like a wounded bobcat struggling to get shed of a trap! Scared me, he did."

Lonnie was brokenhearted over the murder of his sweetheart, but the law would not believe him. He hadn't killed her, he loved her and they were planning to get hitched come summer. How could the law convict him for something he hadn't done? But it was his gun and his girl and that was enough for the sheriff. When the judge delivered the sentence it was fifteen years on the chain gang. Lonnie was enraged for he knew that the real murderer was out there free as a mountain rattler while the best part of his own life would be gone. Sticks and stones can break your bones but words, he thought, yes, words *can* hurt you just the way you'd take a sharp knife to core an apple and throw the core on the ground to rot. That's what had happened to his life.

It was almost a matter of hours from that courtroom to the chain gang.

He could scarcely get out of the big metal cage at the prison camp because of the chain and the steel cuffs around each ankle; and he almost pitched forward on his face when he took his first step. His smile made you feel like smiling back. His eyes crinkled up at the corners when he was amused and his parents never had a lick of trouble with him. If anything he was almost too softhearted and would expend hours trying to nurse an animal back to health when it might just turn out to be a sickly critter at best. Lonnie Stephens didn't act like a killer.

It was his first day on the Alabama chain gang. Gripping the calves of his legs were leather straps meant to hold the steel cuffs up but they still scraped his ankles. The chain between the cuffs was shorter than a man's steps and was designed to keep him from running, but for Lonnie who was a tall fellow with a long stride, every step he took was like being in a sack race with a midget. Alabama had lots of rocks and all he could think about was that he had lots of time ahead of him.

When the man in the next cage passed the chain to him the first night to put through his cuff and hand to the next man he whispered as he turned to him, "Settle down mountain boy. This is a 'hard rock camp' and you just goin' to make it tough for yo'sef." He couldn't sleep well at first because each time a man moved during the night the chain tugged everybody else on the line. But he got used to it and to getting up with the men before daylight.

He tried to join the others as they sung—"Wa-a-ater boy. Where are a you hidin'. If you don' 'a come, gonna fetch yo', mammy." And then the faster chorus. "Gonna hit that rock, boys, from here to Macon, from heah to Macon. . . . " At first he didn't join in but soon he knew why the caged men sang. While they were working on the roads, singing was the only thing that seemed to ease the feeling of hurt inside.

In the middle of the day the guards handed out cans of beans and the water boy came around with a dipper. The sun moved higher and higher overhead as he broke rock with the sledge hammer and rolled it to the pile with his bare hands. His shirt was drenched in perspiration and began to stick to his skin. Late that afternoon he left his sledge hammer where he was breaking rock and went over for a drink of cool water.

"Hey! You biggety mountain boy. Don' you know to ask for water? See that stake? Get over there!" His hands were tied high near the top of the stake and he saw one of the sunburned, stubble-faced guards standing spread-legged in front of him with a wide leather belt that had holes in it. "Take that shirt off'n him," ordered the guard. Sometime during the whipping Lonnie fainted. When he came to, the water boy was throwing water

on his face and his back hurt like nothing he'd ever felt before.

He moaned throughout the night. As soon as his back got well enough and he could think about something besides the pain he made up his mind he was going to either escape or be killed trying. While they were working on the road they could look down in the valley and along the sides of the mountain and see the cabins with their blue chimney smoke drifting up. His friend, Vester, said "Them ain't like other folks. They'll look out after us an' holp us ef we can git there."

A week later Lonnie was in his cage trying to read the only thing he had been able to bring with him. It was a small Bible Cordelia had given to him after he had declared his intention to marry her. A guard named Guthrie entered his cage and he looked up in surprise. "Take your dirty hands off'n the Bible. You ain't fit to touch it, you murderin' bastard," said he and he kicked it out of Lonnie's hands. Lonnie didn't say anything out loud but his mouth moved as he cursed Guthrie wordlessly and he reached to pick it up.

Guthrie promptly sent him to the "hole." Some of the prisoners called it the "box" because it was the severest form of punishment reserved for those who defied a guard. The box had a hard, rough, wooden floor and was fitted inside with chains. It was less than five feet by five feet—too short to stand in and not long enough to lie down in. Twice a day they brought Lonnie a slice of bread and a cup of water. The only thing he knew he could do to keep from going crazy in the horrible discomfort and darkness was to put his mind on something else. Lonnie thought about Branch Corey. He knew Corey had taken a fancy to Cordelia and that the man was infuriated because she had rejected him.

Lonnie was sure that Corey had killed Cordelia and set it up so Lonnie would be blamed.

Lonnie thought about somehow tollin' him down to the creek where Corey had kilt Cordelia and then chokin' him real slow. Didn't make no difference if they hanged him for it. It would be better 'n spending the time on the chain gang. Then he began to think more calmly about how he could establish his own innocence and get evidence that would convict Branch Corey.

After that first day in the hole, he calmed down some and knew he could never kill anybody. But if his lawyer and members of his family hadn't found any clues to convict Corey, he would bring him to justice himself. He knew during his trial that the murder weapon had his initials on it and did look like one of his guns. Branch Corey had admired a gun of his the fall before and asked if he could shoot it sometime. He had offered it to him then. Had he gotten someone to copy the gun and scratched the initials on it himself? If he had only told his lawyer about this during the trial. It was dumb not to think of it for it had happened almost a year ago, about the time he began seeing Cordelia. Ah. That was it! Even then Corey probably began to think about what he would do to get revenge.

He realized now that this confinement with no distractions was ideal for another purpose. He would spend it on something else just as important—figuring out the details of his escape. He could fade back into the mountains and never be caught by the law. Mountain folk were clannish and even if the law suspected he was up there somewhere, they might decide it wasn't worth the risk to come and get him. One of his own family might be able to track down who made the copy of his gun and indict Corey, powerful as he was in the area.

Gradually his escape plan took shape. Vester and another friend named Thurmond could help. They would be working on that mountain road and one day they would reach the right curve. The right curve would be where the front guard leading the line of fifty or sixty prisoners couldn't see far behind him. He could see the whole thing in his mind, the guard foreman walking in the middle alongside the men who would be spread out as they went around the curve.

On the hard wooden floor in the pitch black darkness of the hole the days crawled past but by the morning of the seventh day when he was to get out, he had planned everything down to the last detail. They would overpower the guard foreman, take his pistol and then keep him in front of the men. The guard in front wouldn't be able to shoot for fear of hitting the foreman. They'd shoot the guard in front in the legs if he didn't throw them his gun right off; and then they'd be gone. It had to happen fast for guards working men "under the gun" never aimed a warning shot, they always shot to kill.

An opportunity came less than a week after Lonnie was out of the hole and back on the chain gang again. The men were out working on Alabama Highway 11. It was late afternoon and Lonnie looked down to see blood on his shoe. The leg irons had begun to cut into the flesh on one ankle but he disregarded it. Each day Lonnie and Vester had managed to station themselves about mid-way along the column. Today, the lead guard happened to be Guthrie whom Lonnie hated and, as usual, the foreman was patrolling about halfway up the line of men

The front third of the strung-out prisoners had rounded the curve when Lonnie gave the signal. Vester who was a big, strong man in his early thirties jumped the foreman. But the blow to the guard's head did not prevent him from letting out one terrified yell for help.

It was heard by Guthrie but it alerted the prisoners, too, and since they knew the plan they had the advantage and were able to fall back quickly before the startled Guthrie realized what was happening. When he did, he was looking squarely into the foreman's gun aimed at him by Lonnie.

"I ain't shot squirrel and deer all my life for nothin' Guthrie," he called out. "Throw me your gun."

Guthrie hesitated, then threw it short of Lonnie and to one side. When Lonnie went for it, Guthrie charged him. There was the sound of a shot and the guard fell back dead. They took his keys. With a desperate, hobbling gait the men reached the prison bus. The old bus sped down the mountain road with Vester at the wheel driving as fast as he used to when he was running liquor. In about fifty miles they were almost out of gas and there was nothing to do but abandon the bus in the woods. Several of the men had files and one of Guthrie's keys had worked on most of the leg chains except for

Vester's. They needed to fan out to cabins in the area and find a change of clothes. In the truck tool box, Lonnie discovered a file and began using it quickly to free his friend.

Through the trees they could see the highway they had just left and as Lonnie filed hurriedly, they saw the prison camp truck pass. There go the "dog boys" said Vester. These were the prisoners the men reserved their deepest contempt for, the ones who helped the guards run down escapees.

"We better light out and go different ways, Vester. How much time we've got depends on how far down the road they let 'em out. Them dogs are gonna be confused for awhile by all the trails but then they'll settle down."

"You still got your prison suit on, Lonnie."

"Somebody will help me. I may even get a lift," and with his long legs at last free of the cruel shackles, Lonnie ran off alone through the woods in the gathering darkness.

Bob and Sandy Burns were married in her church in Decatur just as she had always wanted, despite the depression and hard times. It was September of 1935 and she and her husband of several hours were driving up Highway 11 in a borrowed Model A for a brief honeymoon at the Reed House in Chattanooga. The wedding had been at five, the reception at six, and now it was past eight as the car's headlights pierced the darkness north of Fort Payne. For late September, the evening was warm and Bob opened the front window.

On the old Model A Fords, the windshield could be opened and pushed forward on a hinge so that a space of several inches at the bottom sucked in the oncoming air and circulated it over driver and passenger. Sandy held her head back enjoying

the cool night air flowing across her face. Bob pushed the gas pedal down more, for there were no other cars on the road tonight and he would be glad to arrive at the Reed House where he had made their reservation. They would finally be away from all the festivities, which both agreed had continued for almost too long.

Bob pressed the accelerator and the car gained speed. A mist was rolling in across the highway to give the landscape an almost otherworldly look for even the most familiar objects can be eerie at night when the ground fog rises. Sandy put her head on his shoulder and gave a little sigh of pleasure, for the stress of wedding preparations was over and she was thinking that the rest of the night belonged to them. But her pleasure was short lived. As the Model A's headlights swung around the curve, they both saw it at the same time.

As his foot hit the brakes Bob knew he had been going too fast and he also knew that if the figure didn't move out of the road he would hit it. There stood someone full in the path of his car reaching with arms outstretched toward them. As they approached they could see the tall figure of a man dressed in the black and white stripes of prison garb, his clothes tattered as if torn from running through heavy brush. But it was the face they were both riveted to for the expression did not look like that of a criminal. It was young with an imploring look and the way the mouth moved, Sandy was sure she could understand the words—"Help me!"

Time seemed to go into slow motion and every second was endless. The brakes were slowing the car but they were not slowing it fast enough and as the distance narrowed to a few feet, then inches— the figure just stood there making no effort to move. Bob braced himself for the impact and Sandy closed her eyes.

The car's bumper hit the figure but there was not the slightest jolt. Instead a huge, dark shadow rose up from the pavement and like the flow of air over the front hood, literally glided up the windshield. Sandy felt the wind flowing under the open glass turn icy cold and for a second it was as if part of the misty figure was being sucked in with the air! For an instant she felt faint. Astounded, Bob looked in the rear view mirror to see the man now standing behind the car still holding out his arm in the same beseeching appeal for help.

He slowed the Ford and pulled off the road to a stop and got out. There were no other cars in sight and he could just make out the figure in the red glow from the tail light. Then, in the distance, Bob heard the barking chorus of hound dogs as if on a chase and he turned his head in the direction of the sound. When he looked back there was no one to be seen. Sandy was at his side. The pair stood there in the damp, cool air with the barks of the dogs floating on it from afar. Then the yelps faded and an almost palpable quiet enveloped them.

There was nothing to do but to return to the car and continue their trip. The lights of the city would be a welcome sight, thought Sandy. Perhaps the excitement of the wedding had been too much. And then she spoke for the first time.

"Why did we stop, Bob?" He gave her an incredulous look.

"You know perfectly well why we stopped. We stopped because of the man there in the road. Didn't you see him?"

"Yes. I saw him but it was so strange I was beginning to doubt my senses."

"You thought we were both over tired but I'm not so tired that I've begun seeing men in striped prison clothes in the road."

"I know. I saw what he had on, too."

The next morning the Reed House delivered a bountiful Sunday breakfast to their room and a copy of the morning paper. Sandy was munching on a blueberry muffin as she read the headlines.

Then she saw the story. "Was This Man Innocent?" the bold headline asked, and beneath it she read, "Killed on Highway 11 in Alabama while attempting to escape; authorities now think Lonnie Stephens may have been innocent. It happened just a year ago last night. . . ." Sandy put down the paper. She recalled the imploring look on the face they had seen and now she knew what it meant.

Nor was this the only time people have seen the apparition of Lonnie Stephens on Highway 11, the mountain boy whose vindication finally came, but too late to save his life.

Fort Mountain

Fort Mountain, Georgia

Frank Willard decided that if he continued to go over in his mind the reasons the stock market had fallen, he still wouldn't know any more than any other broker. He just wanted to get away from Atlanta, to go where it would be peaceful and beautiful and that meant the mountains of North Georgia. He and Meg and their seven-year old daughter Sarah would stay in a cabin tonight rather than outdoors; because it was Friday and it took time to set up camp. But tomorrow night they would sleep under the stars on Fort Mountain.

"Dad, why are you taking that equipment? I've never even seen you use it before?"

"You haven't, punkin, but I think it may come in handy." He was constantly surprised by how observant Sarah was.

He had found some gear that he had used during his college years and he wanted to recapture the freedom from worry he had known more than a decade ago before the world grew so complicated. Not only had he lost much of his client's money but some of his own as well, for he believed in what he recommended and usually bought the same stocks for himself. North Georgia was one of his favorite places and he was looking forward to getting there, although the place they were staying tonight was a small cabin over a century old and very primitive. It was near Chadsworth. "Use it whenever you and your family want to get away," a friend had generously told him.

He was lucky that Meg and young Sarah were both good campers and seemed to enjoy it as much as he did. They reached the cabin about nine o'clock that night and were ready for bed. When they went in, he led the way with his flashlight and then it went out. "Don't worry, Dad, I've got mine," said Sarah and she handed it to him so Meg could light a candle. In a little while they had two kerosene lamps burning and Frank could see the log walls and an old fireplace with smoky stones across the top. What a musty odor the place had he thought and he doubted anyone had lived there in years.

There was no running water, just a pump on the back porch and he really didn't want to chance drinking from it. They washed their faces out at the pump and he and Sarah refreshed themselves with spring water from one of the jugs.

They were in bed in less than thirty minutes, when he was awakened by Sarah's voice coming from off in the distance saying, "Daddy, I can't sleep."

"You'll be asleep in a few minutes, honey," he replied.

A minute or so passed and he had just dozed off when the child's voice spoke up again. "Daddy, it's hard to sleep with all that music going on."

"Music? I don't hear a thing. Meg, do you hear any music?"

"No, I don't. What does it sound like, honey?"

"Well, it's banjoes and fiddles playing and it's out there in the front room."

"Sarah, you're just imagining that."

"No, Daddy. I've heard some of those songs at school but these are prettier."

"Well, you'll just have to enjoy them alone then because Dad and Mom are tired and we're going to sleep."

Next morning everyone slept late because the large trees shaded the cabin from the morning sunlight. They didn't try to cook but ate breakfast at a fast food place in Chadsworth.

"Daddy, when people die can they come back and play the music they used to play?"

"No. When they die they don't come back and play any music."

"Then where did the music come from that I listened to last night?"

"Sarah, I don't want to hear any more about that music. Sometimes you take teasing too far."

"All right, Dad, but. . . ." Her mother frowned at her and Sarah stopped. She looked out the window then and was very quiet.

As they drove up the mountain they could see the tall tulip poplars with their golden leaves fluttering in the breeze, gray trunks straight and tall and the woods on each side of the road were an artist's palette of colors. In the lemon light of Indian summer the dogwoods shook what crimson leaves they had left in a last act of defiance. A squirrel holding a hickory nut stood motionless staring out at the road from the edge of the woods. This was when the seasons turned and as they did there was always this pause, this magical suspension of time that made Frank feel that he and everything around him would go on forever, just as it was at that moment.

"Dad, is it all right if I don't go with you or mother?"

"Why is that?"

"I thought I'd go looking for those little things called British Soldiers that grow on logs or maybe mushrooms."

"That's fine but just don't eat any and don't get lost."

"Dad, when have I gotten lost?" Sarah looked indignant.

"You haven't. But take your compass anyway." And it was true, she had a good sense of direction and after the first few trips they hadn't worried about her at all. She was a pretty remarkable little girl, he thought proudly.

As a boy in his teens Frank loved to come here. It was his special place to get away from parents and other perplexities. Like everyone who sees the wall of stones at the foot of the mountain, he often wondered about the people who built it, "moon-eyed people with blond hair" the Cherokee legends called them. Long before Columbus was born a band of people of Welsh heritage had landed in Mobile Bay and somehow made their way to North Georgia.

The Cherokees had called them the "moon-eyed people" because it was believed that they worshiped the moon. They were also credited with seeing better at night than animals.

The last gold shreds of the dress a tulip poplar had worn since spring drifted down coming to rest on the wall where Frank sat and for the first time he thought about the size of the stones and their weight. Many of them were far heavier than he could pick up alone; and several people would be needed to move them. He visualized the hands that had lifted these stones and wondered about the people who had placed them here so long ago.

Actually a barrier of loosely piled stones, the wall extended almost a thousand feet around one side of the mountain from east to west. It was three to seven feet high and at intervals along it were round, shallow pits encircled by rocks that may have been used as sentry posts or watch fire pits. The legend of the Welsh who came over to this continent in 1170 under the leadership of Prince Modoc had much credibility. They must have thought the Alabama area would be more desirable than Wales, for according to the story part of their group went back to bring more settlers leaving only two hundred behind. Whether by Indian attacks or disease, they dwindled until only a few were left and in an effort to protect themselves they migrated from Alabama up into Georgia until they reached Fort Mountain. Prince Modoc, who had remained behind with his people, ordered them to build a fort which would afford more permanent protection. For weeks they must have patiently carried the stones until finally their European-style line of defense, unlike the wooden stockades of the later English settlers, was completed on the flank of the mountain.

Now they were protected, for the outposts of fire pits illumined the night and any invaders were silhouetted against the sky. Moccasined feet or bare feet would become bloody feet in crossing the barrier of sharp stones which lay in front of the wall and the movement of rocks underfoot ruled out an attack by stealth. After lighting the fires, the Welsh could fall back among the trees and pick off their attackers as they crossed the rocks in the light from the flames.

How long they were able to survive among the Indians is not known, but stories about them and their blue eyes and golden hair continue to echo down through the centuries. Frank thought about how much we rely upon books forgetting those mysterious, mist covered eons before there were written records when the only history of a people's past came down to each successive generation through the memorized stories of the elders of a tribe. They alone transmitted stories of a "great wind" probably a hurricane, a devastating volcanic eruption, the disappearance of an island and its people into the ocean, a great victory in battle, and the deeds of heroic men and women.

Then he thought about another explanation for the wall—the story that de Soto and his men had built it as they hunted for gold on their journey through the southeast. De Soto was here in 1540 but according to what Frank had read about the period, the Spaniard's diaries indicated that they seem to have been in the area near Fort Mountain only about two weeks. Building walls was not the sort of work Spaniards liked and although de Soto would probably have used enforced Indian labor, he was an impatient man and gold was his real objective. This meant constant travel and a stone wall of defense would not have served any real purpose for him. When he interrogated the Indians about gold they often pointed toward the high mountains of Tennessee and North Carolina in an attempt to hurry the Spaniards on their way.

Just after sunset, Meg and Sarah returned from their explorations and water was heated for coffee. Meg had packed sandwiches and made a cake. Sarah found a flat, sheltered place to put her sleeping bag and lay down soon after dark. When Meg and Frank checked on her, the child's blond head rested against the large brown teddy bear she always cuddled at home and her breathing was soft and even. She was almost seven and very mature in some ways, but in others, perhaps, too imaginative, thought Frank. He hoped she would grow out of this fantasizing. At least tonight he would have a good night's sleep. He was emotionally exhausted by the week he had been through and tomorrow he would enjoy sharing his knowledge of the history of the wall with Sarah and Meg.

It was almost midnight when Sarah waked to the rhythmic tones of distant drums. They aren't like the drums I've heard in a parade, she thought. They are almost like notes of music, but somehow, the sound seems old and covered up with moss. The drums grew louder. Sarah put on her shoes and her coat and started in the direction of the strange poly-phony.

To her delight, she saw fireflies out in the for-est over near the wall. She loved chasing them in the summer but this was October and all the fireflies at home in Atlanta were gone. As she drew closer she saw that the flickers of light were not fireflies at all but torches and as they were carried along toward the wall, trees momentarily blocking them from view made them appear to flicker.

Then coming up in the east and in a trajectory with the wall was a light, a huge, pale yellowish-white incandescence, round and so immense she could see the dark places on the surface. It was the largest full moon she had ever seen.

It was almost as bright as if it were just after sunset and about a hundred yards away from her she could see figures wearing animal skins. They reminded her of the cave men pictures she had seen in a book but they weren't all rough and hairy look-ing. Their hair shone as blond in the moonlight as her own and their limbs were white skinned. Now the figures were climbing the wall and walking with a measured tread toward the full moon. Their arms were raised as if in worship and she stood watching hypnotized for it seemed the moon was pulling them toward it.

Then she realized that if she didn't hurry, they would all be gone before she could even speak to one of them! Sarah broke into a run. She had nearly reached the wall when her foot stepped on a loose rock and she tumbled forward hurting her knees and scraping her arms in an effort to protect her face.

When she looked up, she saw the last of the torches flickering out in the darkness like fireflies carried off by the wind. The notes of the drums had ceased.

On Sunday morning Frank Willard waked up feeling greatly refreshed. Soft golden rays of the morning sun sifted through the trees, birds were singing and in every way, it was a brand new day.

He looked over at his family. Meg was just waking up and greeted him with a sleepy smile, but Sarah who was usually up before anyone else lay still in her sleeping bag. Looking at her he couldn't even tell whether she was breathing she seemed in such a deep sleep and for a moment he was worried. He bent over and touched her shoulder.

"Honey, honey. Wake up."

"Who are you!" she cried out.

"What do you mean, who am I, I'm your father."

"Of course, Dad. I know you are. I guess I was just sound asleep." Her father laughed and ruffled the golden waves of her hair with his hand.

Sarah stretched and discovered to her suprise how sore her knees were. Stealing a cautious look at them, she saw they were badly scratched and that where the skin was broken some places were streaked with blood. Her parents would see this if she wore the shorts she had on the day before.

"Daddy, I want to tell you what. . . ." And then she suddenly stopped.

"Yes?"

"Nothing. Nothing important."

She remembered how her father had cut her off the morning before when she began talking about the beautiful music she had heard in the old cabin. Describing what she had seen at the wall might only irritate him. Then he would make her feel foolish by saying she was too imaginative. Sarah reached into her canvas pack and pulled out the pair of blue jeans to cover her injured knees. She would not tell him about the people on the wall—at least not now and maybe never.

The Woman in Black

Smoky Mountains, Tennessee

At first Ila Jeffers thought she was feverish and puny feeling because of the birthin' of Ginny Sue. She was glad midwife, Granny Moss, had come back by the house to check on her and felt all the more grateful since they lived aways up in the cove. Granny had been delivering babies nigh on to thirty years.

The midwife turned up the kerosene lamp and her knowledgeable eyes stared hard at Ila who lay there in the iron bed, her face white as the muslin sheet, her beautiful, shoulder length, silky black hair uncombed and tangled. Granny was worried.

"Your color ain't good, honey. I was lookin' to find you just as chipper as you were after your last young 'un. 'Member how when I come by here 'spectin' to see you lyin' up in the bed and you was out puttin' in taters' the very next afternoon?" Ila nodded weakly and searched Granny Moss's eyes trying to fathom whatever secrets were contained in their green depths. Granny untied a bandana and some small, clear drugstore vials tumbled out, but they didn't contain pills they held herbs.

"I want you to take just a smidgen of this in a cup 'a hot tea every hour, Ila. This is the strongest yarb I ever seed and I was carrying some over the mountain to Nell Lyons, but there's enough for the both of you." Granny put a pinch of the "yarb" in a cup, went over and got the kettle off the top of the wood heater and poured in some hot water. When the liquid in the cup had turned a smoky yellow she handed it to Ila placing one arm behind the slim shoulders to help her sit up.

"Would you fetch Ginny Sue for me, Granny. I hear her fussin'. It's time I was nursin' her." Granny went over to the walnut cradle near the stone fireplace and as she picked up the small bundle, wrapped first in an old flour sack and then in a tiny handwoven wool kiver, the baby grew quiet in her practiced hands.

"I remember layin' Andrew in that cradle twenty-eight years ago. Where is that rascal?"

"Gone into town to buy me some aspirin."

"You shore he didn't go after no white lightnin'?"

"N'om. You know Andrew. He don't drink nor cuss. He's as good a man as a woman ever had." Granny pressed her thin lips together and her head bobbed up and down in agreement.

"That's true. I never heared nothin' but good of Andrew, and he shore were tickled 'bout this little girl. Just walked backards and forards with her in his arms, wantin' to hold her all the time 'til I had to tell him if she war' a little kitten all that handlin' would kill her."

"Granny, what's the matter with Ginny Sue? She's not nursin' good. She's fussin' like she's hungry but turnin' her head away."

"She shouldn't be a'doin' that."

"I'm scared, Granny. You reckon my baby's sick, too?" Ila's blue eyes had tears in them and her lower lip trembled.

"I don't know, Ila, but I'll be back this way tomorrow afternoon and I'll look in on ye and the baby."

"Ef it don't discomfit ye none, Granny." Ila looked up at her gratefully.

Granny hadn't gone over a mile before she met Andrew in his pick-up truck. He waved to her to stop and she pulled her old blue Plymouth toward the outside of the one lane road while he parked close to the mountainside. He read her face.

"She's bad off, ain't she Granny?"

His eyes looked anguished, then the line of his jaw hardened and he shook his head.

"It's chancy. We'll just have to wait and see."

"Yes, wait and see."

"Now, if you could get Dr. Curry to come up here."

"I went by his place. He's gone to Asheville and won't be back until late tomorrow afternoon. Can't you help her any?"

"I left her some of my medicine, Andy. I'm goin' to stop to see Ila on my way back from Union

Camp area." But she didn't get back the next day because Nell Lyons went into labor and the baby didn't arrive until late that night. She stayed on at the Lyons's house two more days which Granny almost never did, but Nell was quite weak. Will Lyons was mighty good with cattle but he didn't know much about how to help take care of a new baby.

The morning after Granny left, Will was down at the barn before daylight milking the cows. As it began to grow light he was surprised to see the slim figure of a woman in a black dress silhouetted against the doorway of the barn. Her features were not visible in the semi-darkness and there was nothing familiar about her appearance. When he spoke she held her head down and made no reply. Then she was standing beside him and noticing the woman had a cup in her hand, he asked her if she would like some milk. She held it out to be filled but left without thanking him or saying a word. Early next morning at about the same time, she came into the barn once more.

"Good morning," he said, but she did not reply. Once more he filled her cup and he thought he saw her nod gratefully, but she still did not speak. Blackberry winter was what the mountain folk called this unseasonably cold weather in May and because of that he took notice that she did not have a coat on over her dress. He told Nell about it when he went back to the house and she said it might be one of the neighbor girls come over because their cow had gone dry.

At the little cabin on the other side of the mountain, Ila seemed to be a little stronger the evening after Granny Moss had left her the herbs. Andrew prepared steaming hot tea for her and each time when she drank it she would say she felt better. The baby, however, was still not nursing the way she had at first and his wife thought Andrew should fetch the doctor as soon as he returned. By morning Ila, herself, had taken a turn for the worse. She was flushed and feverish, tossing, moaning and too delirious even to hold her baby, Ginny, who now lay listlessly in the cradle.

Why wasn't Granny Moss back? That morning Andrew drove down the road a piece thinking he might see her and make sure she came up to the cabin, but there was no sign of Granny. When he returned he first thought his wife was asleep, then he realized she was dead. Within an hour the baby girl gave a little cry and breathed her last. Then great, harsh sobs began to rack his thin shoulders and he flung himself across the bed beside his dead wife. He must have fallen asleep for the next thing he knew someone was pounding on the door.

It was Granny Moss and the doctor.

"Andrew, I thought that wife of your'n needed him so I went back by way of his house and brought him, how is. . . ."

"You're too late."

She saw the agony on his face and fell silent. Andrew stepped back to let them in. The doctor went over to the bed first, looked down at Ila and didn't even bother to take her pulse.

"Where's the baby, Andrew?"

"Hit's in the crib."

He picked up the limp little form and then, very gently, laid her back in the cradle. I doubt I could have done anything even if I'd been here. Everbody that's had this fever has been mighty sick with it, and I thought we'd lose more folks than we did. Andrew, I'm sorry as I can be."

The funeral was held the next afternoon in the little cemetery on top of a nearby hill. Blackberry winter was still here and a cold, gray day it was, with a mizzling sort of rain. It put Andrew in mind of the day of his father's funeral the winter before; how Ila had stood next to him strong and comforting but now, she too was gone and he was all alone. The loss of the baby hurt for they had looked forward to it together, but he had never suffered anything like the pain he felt over losing Ila.

"Oh death where is thy sting, oh grave where is thy victory . . ." the preacher's voice intoned and as he heard those words pronounced to comfort so many over the years, a vast rage engulfed him. He knew Ila and their child were in heaven and beyond any more suffering—but what about him? Didn't God care anything about him? What did he, Andrew, have left! He had never felt as close to the Lord as his wife had always seemed to be and today—not at all. Andrew raised the collar of his overcoat up around his neck to shield himself from the wind; but the worst chill of all was inside him and it took every ounce of his determination to keep from shaking. Lord, he felt like he was freezing to death and it was inside him.

Will and Nell Lyons talked about how sad it was and how bad Andrew was looking.

"Time's a great healer, Will," said his wife and Will wondered how some women always had a saying to cover things no matter how bad they were. And then he remembered that even after the harshest winter, ice melts, there are warm breezes, trees bloom, spring comes. Maybe his wife was right.

Next morning he was going about his milking and when the cow turned her head and mooed, he looked in that direction. There came the girl dressed in black and she was holding out the cup just as she had done on the other two occasions.

"Good-morning," he said cheerfully, but no reply came. He didn't try to talk to her any more and she stood there without a word while the only sound was that of the warm, fresh milk spurting and the ping as it hit the inside of the tin cup. He decided that this morning he was going to follow her at a distance and see if he could find out where she went. As she left the barn he rose from his milking stool and quietly walked after her. It was a pewter gray sky now instead of black and he could see the dark, slim form seemingly glide along ahead of him as they crossed the pasture, he about fifty feet behind her. On she went through the brush around the side of Big Bear Mountain with Will following. He worried that a careless step along the path might start some of the small, loose rocks rolling and he would be discovered.

The sun would be up in a few minutes and then, if she looked back, she would surely see him for now they emerged from the woods. She took the muddy little road that led up the back way to the top of the hill and walked at such a pace that Will could scarcely keep up with her, but by now he knew her destination. This was the road the gravediggers sometimes used and across the top of the hill was the community cemetery. For the first time he began to feel uneasy. Why was she on her way to the graveyard?

He was surprised to see the cemetery gate standing half open and through it she went, only stopping to pull it closed behind her. He thought then she would see him for certain but although she turned and was facing him, she didn't appear to be aware of his presence. He followed her only a few feet further and then stopped hidden from view behind a large tulip poplar. As he watched, the girl walked over to a grave and as he peered between the stones, she vanished. Shocked and incredulous, Will still did not doubt what he had seen. On the way home, and this time he took the main road, he saw Jake Jackson rattling along in his old truck. He hailed him.

"I'm on my way to set out a load of new Christmas tree seedlings. You want to help?"

"Jake, I need help myself. How about turning around."

"I got work to do. Where you want to go?"

"To the cemetery."

"Cemetery!"

"Yes. You got a shovel on this truck?"

"Sure do." Something in Will's expression made him turn around and they headed up the hill. When they reached the graveyard, Will went around to the back of the truck and got the shovel. "Can you find another?"

"Just this small one."

"Well, bring it along." He led the way over to a freshly dug grave at the edge of the cemetery.

"Why this is Ila Jeffer's grave. She died of the fever only a few days ago. We can't go diggin' her up."

"I got good reason for this, Jake. Now, don't be squeamish and just give me a hand." As the hole grew wider and deeper they began to hear a faint sound. They dug faster, throwing the dirt up furiously around the edge of the grave. The sound grew louder and became a whimper punctuated by cries. When they reached the coffin, Will knelt down and tore the lid clean off. There in the coffin lay Ila Jeffers in a black dress but she was not alone. In the crook of one arm rested her baby.

"Lord, a mighty! This baby's alive," cried out Will. The baby was crying and those were the sounds the men had heard as they were digging. Will reached into the coffin to pick up the baby and as he did, his fingers touched something else. Beside the mother's hand was the metal milk cup he had filled that morning.

Andrew Jeffers had not built a fire nor had a bite to eat for two days. His girl, Cindy, who had been visiting her aunt in West Virginia had come home the night before and been pressing him to eat some of the food folks had brought. He was about to leave the little cabin to cut fresh wood for the stove when he saw a truck heading up the road toward his house. His hand reached for his shotgun when his daughter spoke up. "Quit that, Daddy. It's Mr. Jackson's truck." Then he recognized it as the Jackson Tree Farm truck. The men drove up near the porch and when Andrew went out and heard the cries of a baby, he thought they were up to some kind of strange carrying on, and his face grew red with anger.

"Wait, before you holler at us, Andy. We ain't meanin' to hurt you none," said Will Lyons. "We've brought something for you. This is your own baby.

Don't tell me how bad the Lord's done treated you now."

It was a miracle, a real miracle, said everyone. And the story of the mother whose spirit somehow managed to return to care for her baby can still be heard in that part of the Tennessee mountains not far from the North Carolina line.

Laura

Campbellsville, Kentucky

The afternoon was gray and misty, not the kind that Larry Huff would usually choose for a motorcycle ride. But he had just traded in his old motorcycle for a new Honda—bought himself a new jacket—and the temptation to take off was irresistible.

When he sped down Highway 55 out of Campbellsville, Kentucky, and headed south toward Columbia, he had no premonition of what lay in store for him.

It was a great ride, with the cool, moist air blowing in his face as he swooped around the curves. There were almost no cars on the road. In fact, he must have gone five miles before he met one. In some places the fog made it difficult to see for any distance ahead but there were often foggy places along this road and Larry didn't really mind. It gave him a feeling of being in another world—a world of fluffy whiteness and, above all, quiet. He liked that, for in the small house where he lived with his parents and four brothers and sisters, there was often so much noise that there was no chance to think. He wasn't sure just what it was that he wanted to be alone to think about, but sometimes he grew angry inside when the clamor of voices made his thoughts so jerky that he couldn't make sense out of whatever was gnawing on him at the moment. He could put things together when he rode alone like this.

Instead of the weather clearing, a slow, drizzling rain began to fall, but Larry still did not want to turn back. As he rounded one of the curves, a small, single tree near a clump of trees on his right appeared to move. But when he approached, he saw it was a thin-looking girl wearing a cloak walking beside the road.

He stopped to ask if there was anything he could do for her, she looked so cold and forlorn, her hair clinging wetly about her cheeks, her dress long and bedraggled. At first he thought she was not going to answer, but she replied, "Well, if you don't mind, I'd like to have a ride down the road a piece to my house." By now the drizzle had changed to a light rain and Larry offered her his new jacket. She put it on gratefully and climbed up behind him on the motorcycle, winding her arms about his waist. He was conscious of the cold from her hands penetrating even through his shirt. The ride was not a comfortable one as her grip gradually grew tighter, and his back felt cold as ice.

They were near Cane Valley when she spoke up and pointed to a house set back from the highway. "That's where I live," she said and Larry turned up the road toward it. It was an old farmhouse and the girl muttered a quick, "Thank you," ran up the front steps and in the door, closing it behind her. Larry was so glad not to have her holding on with those cold hands around his waist that he hurriedly took off.

It was not until he was part way home that he remembered his new jacket, but by then it was getting quite dark and he had no desire to return to the farmhouse at night.

Next morning he headed back down Highway 55 toward Cane Valley and when he reached the

girl's house he went up and knocked on the front door, thinking she might answer it. A woman came to the door instead, so he described the girl and said he had lent her his jacket.

The woman's eyes filled with tears. "I don't know how you've done it. You've described just how my girl, Laura, looked, but she's been dead seven years."

Larry stared at her in disbelief. "Ma'am, I just can't believe it. She was as real as can be and I could even feel how wet and cold she was."

"Wait a minute. I'd like for you to go with me," said the woman. She went into the house and got her coat and he followed her to the back and up to the top of a hill where there was a small family cemetery surrounded by a fence. As she opened the gate, he was surprised to see something was hanging over the top of a tombstone on the far side.

When they reached it he was amazed. His jacket was draped over the tombstone and below it, engraved on the stone, was the name "Laura." The date was seven years ago. He reclaimed the jacket but it was too damp to put on, even if he had wanted to.

Although he kept the coat for several years, he never seemed able to wear it, for always, after he had worn it for a few minutes, it would begin to feel cold and wet and he would have to take it off. The jacket still looked like new but finally one night, after trying again to wear it, he became angry and threw it in the fire.

A strange odor suffused the room like the scent of flowers massed around a freshly dug grave. Larry was so terrified he ran out of the house into the night.

Even now as he tells the story, his face turns white, his eyes fill with horror and he will never ride down Highway 55 on a foggy, rainy day again.

The Coming of the Demon

Middleway, West Virginia

Adam Livingstone was an honest, religious man and a hard-working farmer. It is hard to realize how a man like this can become involved with a demon, and yet that is what happened.

Near the beginning of the nineteenth century Livingstone and his wife came down to what later became West Virginia from Pennsylvania and purchased a lakeside farm near the town that is now Middleway. It was then called Smithfield and later Wizard Clip. This last name came from the series of disasters that happened to the Livingstone family.

In front of their farm and beside the Opequon River ran the wagon route from Baltimore to southwest Virginia, Kentucky, and Tennessee. During the day, wagon after wagon rattled along the road and Livingstone would sell or barter his farm produce with the wagon drivers.

One bitterly cold November night the event befell the Livingstones that was to lead to a terrifying series of happenings, although it appeared quite commonplace at the time. During these days there were few inns with accommodations for travelers and they often stopped at a house and asked if they might spend the night.

The Livingstones were in bed listening to the rain and wind outside when they heard a pounding on their front door. Adam went down to see who it could be. He cautiously opened the door a few inches but the force of the wind was such that it tore the door from his hand and flung it open revealing a black hole in the outer darkness. In the midst of it stood a tall stranger, his cloak billowing in the wind.

"My wagon wheel is broken and I am not able to have it repaired until morning," said the stranger. "I would like to ask for a night's lodging, sir, and I assure you I will pay you generously."

"We have an extra room and you are welcome to it," replied Livingstone. "My wife has gone to bed or I would ask her to prepare food for you, but let me show you to your room."

The stranger appeared grateful and followed him up the steep, winding stairs to a room which was sparsely furnished but had a comfortable feather bed. Although he wore the clothes of a gentleman, Livingstone took his usual precaution of locking the door at the foot of the stairs. This was a common practice when a family lodged strangers on the second floor for the night.

The Livingstones heard the man walk about the room. They heard his boots hit the floor one by one and then the bed creaked. Leaving only the candle burning by their bed, they were soon asleep. A short time later they were awakened by the sound of a terrible moaning and groaning above them, punctuated now and then by a sharp outcry of pain. It was the traveler.

Taking the bedside candle, Livingstone unlocked the door to the stairs and went up to see what was the matter. He found his guest tossing in his bed and deathly ill. The man told him he did not expect to live to see daylight, and he asked if Livingstone would summon a Catholic priest to give him the last rites, admitting that he had neglected his

religion in health but now felt need of its consolation.

Livingstone told him that there was no priest nearby nor could he hope to find one closer than Maryland but that he would ask his neighbors, the McSherrys and the Minghinis, who were Catholic and perhaps they could tell him of one. Mrs. Livingstone had come up, and as she listened to the conversation she began to grow angry.

"Surely, you are not going out on any such wild-goose chase on a night like this. The best thing we can do is go back to bed, and I'll wager this guest of ours will be as well as you or I by morning."

But the Livingstones could not sleep the rest of the night, for there were the most pitiful cries and pleas coming from the room above. Finally, just before day came, all was quiet. About eight o'clock when they heard no sound, Livingstone went up. Their guest was dead. It was then that they realized they did not know his name and couldn't find it in any of his belongings. Mrs. Livingstone told the neighbors a traveler had asked to lodge with them the night before and had died in his sleep. She did not mention his begging them to summon a priest. The funeral was a simple one, held late the following afternoon.

After the Livingstones returned to their home, Adam built a fire and they sat down before it to warm themselves. Suddenly, the logs in the fireplace began to writhe and twist so violently that they erupted from the fireplace into a fiery dance around the room. Livingstone ran from one to the other trying to catch them and put them back but as soon as he did they would fly out again. When the dancing finally stopped, the Livingstones were too frightened to sleep.

Tired as Livingstone was, he went down to the road with some of his produce the next morning and was surprised to hear a wagon driver cursing at him. The man's team of oxen had stopped in the middle of the road.

"Take that rope down! What are you doing, tying a rope across a public road?" the angry man shouted. The exhausted and bewildered Livingstone could see no rope at all and thought the man must be drunk. The driver took out a large knife and began slashing the air with it. To his amazement the knife met no resistance. Livingstone suggested that he drive on. He did and the wagon went through. What a shame for a man to be drunk so early in the day, thought Livingstone. It was only a short time, however, before another wagon came clattering down the road with a load of pots and pans and the same thing happened. The driver pulled to a stop so quickly that several of the pans fell banging and rattling to the ground. Then he started to shout about a rope, and shook his fist at Livingstone. Finally, he was persuaded to drive on, but similar incidents kept up for several weeks.

By now the Livingstones and their neighbors, who had all noticed these strange events, were sure that they were the work of some supernatural power. Each day brought new and frightening phenomena. Showers of stones would strike the Livingstone house, articles of furniture would topple over, balls of fire rolled over the floor without any apparent cause. But most frequent was a sharp clipping noise as if made by gigantic, invisible shears which could be heard in and around the house, and crescent shaped slits began to appear in the family clothes and table linen.

Mrs. Livingstone and a lady visitor were sitting on the porch talking and the lady commented on the fine flock of ducks waddling through the yard on the way to the river. She had no sooner spoken than the uncanny, invisible shears went "Clip-clip, clip-clip!" and one after another each duck's head fell to the ground before the horrified ladies' eyes.

The young men of the neighborhood talked Livingstone into letting them hold a dance at his home. One boastful fellow brought his rifle and bragged about all he would do if "the Clipper" came near him. For a while everything went smoothly, but right in the middle of one of the dances the fellow who had been boasting began yelling wildly. There was the sound of huge, demoniacal scissors whacking through cloth. The boaster grasped his britches which were now flapping around the back of his legs and ran through the nearest door.

That night, after the dance was over, Livingstone had a strange dream. He dreamed he was standing at the foot of a hill looking up at a man in flowing black robes who was conducting a religious ceremony. As he watched, a voice spoke saying, "I am the man who can rid you of the demon." He was much astonished and decided the man in his dream was a priest so he decided to attend Catholic services nearby at Sheperdstown. He went with his Catholic neighbors, and the moment he saw the

After the demon arrived, the field behind the Livingstone home seemed always to be shrouded in fog.

priest he recognized the man he had seen in his dream.

Tears streaming down this face, he poured out the story of his heartless treatment of the stranger, the weird chain of events that had followed, and he begged for help. Father Cahill was a big-fisted Irishman who was not afraid of the devil himself and he accompanied Livingstone back home. There he got down on his knees and prayed, and sprinkled holy water on the threshold of the house.

"Now, I want you to take me to the place where the stranger was buried," said the priest, and together they went to an old cemetery. Livingstone showed him the grave and the priest began to consecrate it. As he did so, the wind rose, leaves rustled, and small trees started to sway. But along with the wind sounds there was another that grew and swelled until it became a dreadful sort of moan. Livingstone was terribly frightened. He looked at the dark waters of the nearby lake tossing tumultuously. In a few minutes the moan faded and the waters grew still, perhaps, because they had taken back their own.

After that day, there were no more signs of the demon at the Livingstone home, and Adam Livingstone was so grateful that he deeded thirty-four acres of his farm to the Catholic church. The deed may be seen today, recorded on the yellowing pages of an old book in the County Clerk's office at Charles Town, West Virginia. The land is a half mile or so west of the main turnpike through Middleway. The soil is poor, and shattered limestone rock is close to the surface. For many years the foundation of an ancient house could be seen. Many have claimed to hear the hoof beats of a galloping horse there, and on dark and blustery autumn nights they talk of a figure in a billowing cape striding toward the small chapel, built on the spot by the Catholic church, and disappearing within. Is it the spirit of the stranger returning to give thanks at being released from this earth by the priest? No one really knows.

The Letter

South Mountain, Maryland

James Ramsay stood in the fading sunlight. He was surrounded by the bodies of the Confederate dead and, who knows, perhaps their spirits. The battle of South Mountain was over, for the Confederates had come out of a thin line of woods scarcely two hours before, helpless and with empty muskets. His own New York regiment, taking cruel advantage of the situation, had shot them down as they stood there not twenty feet away.

Most of the dead Confederates were from the coastal district of North Carolina. They wore "butternut" uniforms, the color ranging all the way from deep coffee-brown to the whitish brown of ordinary dust. He looked down into the poor, pinched faces, worn with marching and scant fare and his anger toward them died. There was no "secession" in those rigid forms nor in those fixed

eyes staring blankly at the sky. It was not "their" war anymore.

Some of the Union soldiers were taking the finer powder from the cartridge boxes of the dead and priming their muskets with it. Except for that, each body lay untouched as it had fallen. Darkness came on quickly before there was time to bury the dead. Ramsay and his comrades unrolled the blankets of the rebels and went about covering each body. The air was full of the fragrance of pennyroyal, an herb bruised by the tramping of a hundred feet, and he would always remember it as part of this day.

It was Sunday, September 14, 1862, but the air was chilly, and after munching on some of their cooked rations and listening to the firing which continued until about nine o'clock that evening, the men drew their blankets over them and went to sleep. It was a strange sight, thought Ramsay. Stretched out here in the narrow field lay living Yankee and dead Confederate, side by side, nor could one be told from the other.

Sometime after midnight, James Ramsay awoke very thirsty. He reached for his water flask to find it empty, and then he recalled that he had forgotten to fill it at the stream. He must have said this aloud to himself for the figure next to him rose on one elbow and extended his own water flask. Ramsay drank from it gratefully, thanked him, and was about to lie back upon his arms when a voice said, "I have a letter in my breast pocket. Would you see that it gets to my wife?"

"Of course," replied Ramsay, and exhausted he fell asleep once more. He awoke at daylight as he

had for so many dawns during the past few months and began to recall where he was and what had happened the day before while he waited for the rest of the camp to stir. Then he remembered his buddy next to him who had given him a drink during the night. What was it the man had said? He had asked him to carry a letter to his wife, that was it. Poor fellow. Like all of them, he knew that each day might so easily be his last. Ramsay glanced over at him curiously to see who it was.

Then he realized that the man on his right was not from his own regiment but was one of the dead Confederates they had not had time to bury the night before. It must be the fellow asleep on the other side, then. He turned. This, too, was a dead Confederate. Nor was there any water flask on the body.

He could not believe his eyes. He was certain it had been no dream for he clearly remembered the man raising up to give him water. One thing would tell him. He peeled the blanket back from the Confederate and reached into his breast pocket. In it was a letter addressed to "Mrs. John Carpenter." He opened it and began to read: "My dearest wife, I think of you daily and in the event I am not able to return to tell you. I want you to know that . . ."

Ramsay read no further. He was not a superstitious man, but he knew that his experience was too real to discount. He would never forget the night he had met the spirit of a Confederate soldier named John Carpenter as they slept side by side in a field in Maryland.

The Ghost Fiddlers

Hill Country, West Virginia

There is an old house in West Virginia that only comes alive at night. That is, if you can say that a house inhabited by spirits can come "alive."

The old log cabin leaned forward and seemed to stare menacingly. Its supports sagged. A door hung from one hinge. The young couple stood for a moment and stared back. Then the man walked over to look at the steps.

"Pretty good shape. This 'uns a house with good timber and we can make it right."

"Oh, Peter, this old house scares me just to look at it."

"Scares you?"

"Yes, there's something wrong about it. There'll never be anything but sadness in it."

"You're not thinkin' straight, Sarry. Yer family lets the tunes from all that fiddlin' make 'em feel all

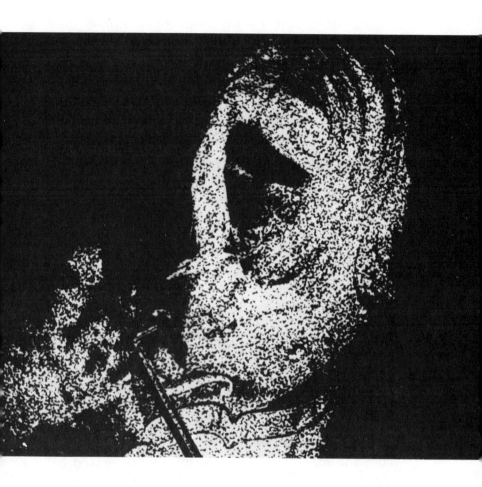

sorts a crazy things. Now, remember, I don't never want none of that fiddlin' in our home."

Sarry's eyes looked hurt, but she gave a reluctant little nod. She was a pretty girl who loved to sing and dance, and she was from a family of fiddle players. The girls could play about as well as the men. But Peter Barton thought the fiddle was an instrument of the devil, for that's the way he was raised. Music led a body away from things they ought to be doing, like serving the Lord, and could make him forget he would soon be standing before the judgment seat.

Peter had wanted to preach but had worked so hard there was no time to practice at it. But my, what a powerful prayer he could make! Lots of folks went to preachin' just to hear Peter Barton pray.

He began to repair the house and sometimes Sarry would come out bringing some of the yellow rosebushes from her homeplace to plant to keep it from looking so desolate.

It was a somber wedding with no music, for Sarry's dad and brothers knew better than to fetch any fiddles along. A year later a boy was born. Peter wanted to call him after one of the thundering prophets of the Old Testament, but Sarry said her grandpappy's name, James, was the same as one of the apostles' and her husband agreed. They lived to themselves, for Peter never wanted to take her over to see her family, for that instrument of the devil, the fiddle, could often be heard, its strains floating from the cabin at night. Secretly, Peter feared he might come to like one of the gay tunes or plaintive lover's ballads and then he was convinced he would lose his faith.

Folks passing the Barton house at suppertime could hear Peter's strong, resonant voice reciting the blessing as if he were giving a benediction to the multitude. He took Sarry and the boy to church and never missed a meeting. People said the prayers he prayed could make chills run down a man's spine.

Somehow, he never had any close friends, for he didn't seem to trust anybody. Some said it was because he'd had to scrabble so hard for what he'd got. They also said he was a strong-tempered man and that both Sarry and the boy were afraid of him.

Sarry's ma took sick one day and they sent for Sarry, so Peter took her and the boy, James, on their two white mules. Right off, James saw a fiddle hanging on the wall and asked his granddaddy what it was for. It was the first time he'd ever seen one. His granddaddy took it down and played a gay, lilting melody. James wanted to try it but his father scowled and the boy was afraid to touch it. When they left, Peter told James that he was never to play such an instrument of the devil and if he ever took it up, he'd have to leave home.

Sometimes Peter would make money by running a raft of logs down the river. There was much timber in the area and he would tie the loose logs into the raft and ride it downstream where he would sell them to buy land. It took about four days because he would have to walk back. One day while he was gone, James's grandmother became sick again and he and his mother went over to the house. He asked his granddad to play for him, and when he had finished James wanted to try it. Sarry's father suggested she take the fiddle home with her and teach the boy while his father was away.

Sarry looked at the fiddle with longing and all the beautiful, haunting melodies she had learned as a girl came to mind. How she had missed them! She couldn't resist, and from then on she and James would play when his father was away.

One morning Peter told them good-by and set out for the river to run a raft of logs downstream and sell the timber.

"The water's pretty high, Sarry, and it may take me longer to get back, for some of the small streams are going to get higher if it rains some more. I may have trouble gettin' acrost them on foot, but I'm aimin' to get back in about four days."

Sarry did her chores. James chopped some wood, planted taters in the garden, and it was late afternoon when he finished. That night after supper his mother saw him look up toward the loft where they had the fiddle hidden. Her eyes met his and she nodded her head, "Go ahead, Jamie." He played while his mother sat listening in the old rocking chair her Pa had given her. Every now and then she would take the fiddle herself and play a tune. The two of them had such a good time they paid no mind to the late hour.

Meanwhile, Peter had set out down the river but the water was high, and about ten miles from home he reached a spot where the river narrowed and curved. Here the current was swift and it pulled the raft right over the big rocks he had always managed to see and avoid when the water was lower. The raft went all to pieces and only by clinging to one of the logs was he able to keep from drowning. He stopped at a house to dry himself and by the time he had walked all the way home, it was getting on toward midnight. He was surprised to see the light of a lamp burning in the little cabin, but as he drew closer he knew why. The wind brought the sound of a gay, foot-tapping melody called

"Sweet Sunny Sal." Peter's face grew grim and hard. The appealing lilt of the tune, rather than touch his heart, only moved him to anger.

A fiddle was used at dances and other frolics. It was clearly the instrument of the devil in the eyes of the mountain preachers, and Peter flung open the door in a black rage. He snatched the fiddle out of Jamie's hands and taking his knife he deliberately cut every string. Then he hung it near the mantel and turned to Jamie, thundering, "There hangs the instrument of the devil as a reminder to all them who would not obey. I told you, Jamie, you'd have to leave this house if you ever brought a fiddle into it. Now, you go to your grandpappy's and stay there."

Jamie had no light, but he was afraid of his father and he left right then. Sarry thought he would go to her Pa's place and stay there 'til Peter cooled down and then come back. But that was not to be.

The following morning Peter rose early to milk the cow. She was in the far pasture and when he went to fetch her, he saw a dark crumpled figure lying at the foot of the cliff at one side of the field. It was Jamie. He had lost his footing in the dark, fallen down the cliff head first, and struck a stump. The boy's neck was broken. Peter carried his son's body back to the house.

It is said that Peter was never the same. He no longer took his logs down the river. He scarcely talked to anyone now, and in church he never prayed aloud again. Four years later he was killed when one of the mules kicked him, splitting his head open. Some folks said he had told Sarry he would live only four years, one year for each string he had cut on the fiddle. He was buried beside his son in the graveyard.

Sarry lived on at the house getting queerer and queerer, and late at night when folks walked the path near the cabin they would hear the strains of a fiddle playing. One morning someone found her sitting in her rocking chair with a fiddle across her

lap and a smile upon her face. Stranger still, even after the old lady died, the sounds kept on and, if anything, there were more and more reports of music rippling through the night air coming from the old cabin, sometimes gay but more often sad and plaintive.

Even today there are few people who care to walk the path near the old cabin after dark, nor does anyone want to stay over night or live there again. It is a dark, sagging skeleton of a place. Yet they say that near midnight the eerie, haunting music of Jamie's fiddle may still be heard—coming from beyond the grave.

The Haunted Copper Mine

Ducktown, Tennessee

Jack McCaulla had worked in the mines all his life and, as his friends used to say, "There ain't much Jack's afeard of." Like every man who worked in the mines, Jack lived with danger, but he knew how to handle it better than most. Or so everyone thought.

The Ducktown copper mines were on the Georgia-Tennessee border and they were the only places a man could make money as good as a dollar a day in the 1890s.

Jack was working a tunnel about four hundred feet down one day when a bunch of men became scared to death. One of the engines failed that ran both the air pump, which pushed fresh air through

the mine, and the wooden elevator that brought men up from the shafts. The miners ran toward the shaft and began scurrying up the steel wire ladder that hung on the solid rock wall, climbing from level to level.

They were all crowded around the base of the ladder and some were pushing and shoving. Just as McCaulla's turn came to go up it, a panic-stricken old man thrust in ahead of him and McCaulla stood aside, letting him go up first. Jack was the last man to go up the ladder. Later his fellow miners talked about it, and when one of the mine officials asked him if it were true, he just said, "Well, we couldn't all climb that ladder at once. Someone always has to be last."

A few months later Jack McCaulla was working about four hundred feet down in the mine when he went to the end of one of the tunnels that had been blasted the day before in a pocket of rich copper-bearing ore. By the light of the lamp on his cap he began to pick up large chunks of the ore and load his mine car with the blasted-down rock.

He had been loading the car for almost an hour when he heard a peculiar hissing sound as if air were escaping from the pipe. The pipes brought the life-saving fresh air under heavy pressure along the tunnels. The sound grew louder and he began to think it might come from water running down the side of the tunnel. He stopped shoveling the ore and began to listen. As he did so he was aware of a change in the sound. No longer was it a hissing nor the noise of running water, but it was becoming more and more eerie.

It was a chorus sobbing and moaning in unison, and he recognized human voices. Somehow, he knew it was the voices of all the miners who had died in this mine and their cries were so loud they seemed to surround and overwhelm him. His hands became clammy, his face beaded with perspiration, and he didn't wait finish loading his mine car but pushed the car to the shaft as quickly as possible. The wailing seemed to follow him all the way to the skip. He rode the skip up, dumped his ore, and went to the surface boss and told him he had heard the cries of all the men who had ever been killed in this mine.

The face of the man who had long been unafraid was the color of ashes. The boss looked at him and paid him off, nor did McCaulla ever go back to work in the Isabella copper mine at Ducktown again.

The Ghost of John Henry Lives On

Talcott, West Virginia

Some people in Talcott, Hilldale, and Hinton, West Virginia, say the ghost of John Henry still haunts the east portal of the Big Bend Tunnel. And it is true that within days after John Henry's death, work came to a halt because laborers could still hear his hammers ringing in the tunnel.

In 1870, when the tunnel was started, John Henry was there. The tunnel was one of the most ambitious projects of its day. More than a mile long, it would cut off nine miles as it went through Big Bend Mountain and came out on the other side. The tunnel was a real man-eater, for the hard, red, shale rock through which it was driven would crumble when exposed to air and at least one out of every five workers died from rock falls in the building of it.

The steel drivers were the princes of the working crews, and John Henry was king of them all. He was a big, black man, six feet tall, two hundred pounds, superbly muscled, and an artist with his hammers. It was not easy to slam one hammer at the end of a 1 1/2-inch-diameter drill hour after hour, day after day without missing.

Little Bill, John Henry's "turner" held the drill turning it slightly after each blow giving it a little shake to flip the rock dust out of the hole. The drills would get dull after a few minutes and while those hammers of John Henry's flew back and forth—he could swing a hammer in each hand—Little Bill would hold out a hand to the "walker" who kept getting the drills resharpened by the blacksmith at the tunnel entrance, and he'd slip another into the hole fast between hammer blows. The steel driver couldn't break the rhythm of his hammers any more than a distance runner could break his stride.

In rock drilling contests the drivers kept up a rate of ninety blows a minute and a dozen times in a fifteen-minute match. The "turner" would replace the steel drill, with bloodied flesh to pay if his timing was poor.

But the most famous contest that ever happened was when John Henry told his boss he could beat the steam drill. John Henry was proud man. The rest of the men admired him and Banks Terry, who used to do odd jobs in the tunnel, always talked a lot about him—said he could drive steel straight ahead or straight into the roof while standing on a powder keg, never tiring, never missing a stroke, singing all the while and wearing out drills as fast as they were brought to him.

The steam drill had not been out long before John Henry thought he'd like to have a match with one.

So John Henry said to the captain:

"A man ain't nothing but a man,
But before I let that steam drill beat me down,
I'll die with my hammers in my hands, Lord, Lord,
Die with my hammers in my hands."

As his hammers flew back and forth ringing through the tunnel, John Henry's body glistened with sweat and shone as though it had been polished. The clang of his hammers was a high, steady chorus even above the sound of the steam drill as this giant of a man pitted himself against the machine. His boss and fellow workers stood watching. There had been some joking with John Henry before the match, but now everyone was silent.

For the first ten minutes the man and the steam drill seemed to be going at about the same pace. Then, little by little, John Henry began to pull ahead. There was one thing in his favor. Every so often the Burleigh drill would clog up on rock dust or hang up in a crack, and while the steam driller was taking care of this, John Henry went right on slinging those hammers—clang, clang, clang.

It was thirty-five minutes before the match was over and by that time John Henry had driven fourteen feet while the steam drill had driven only nine. John Henry turned to the steam driller and said, "Your hole's done choke and your drill done broke." The match was over and John Henry had won. But the big, proud, black man had trouble walking.

"I feel a roarin' and a rollin' in my head," he told Banks Terry, and he staggered home, laid down his hammers, and went to bed. The next morning he was dead. The feelings he had described are the classic symptoms of a stroke and few people nowadays, since the coming of power tools, can imagine such a brutal, man-killing contest.

Later, in 1876 a major rock fall killed a whole train crew, and a brick mason named Alfred Owens was one of those hired by the railroad to work in the tunnel and face it with brick. Owens had lived in the area all his life and been in the tunnel many a time as a boy. It was cold and damp inside it that November afternoon as he hurried to fit the last bricks into an arch and finish before he left. Only a half-dozen bricks remained when he heard a sound in the tunnel. A stray dog, a rat, or worse, a rock fall, for in the great dark voids above the brick arching, blocks of rock shifted and fell with frightening frequency.

He hurried to put the remaining bricks in place, but as he did so, another sound rang out—a clang, clang, clang, clang nearby—and as he looked down the tunnel he saw a shadowy figure in the orange light of his lamp. It was the outline of a huge, strapping man silhouetted near the tunnel opening. In each hand was a hammer and the

immense arms swung with smooth rapidity, never faltering, never losing their rhythm.

Owens was stunned. It was the entrance through which he had planned to leave. He edged toward it, pressing his back close against the tunnel wall while the loud clanging of the hammers striking steel went on and on. The air in the tunnel was cold, but Owens could feel perspiration running down his face. The palms of his hands were damp with fear. He became too frightened to move. A rock dislodged itself near his head and struck his shoulder, but even this did not frighten him nearly as much as the awesome figure swinging the hammers completely unmindful of him.

Then his foot slipped on the wet rock of the tunnel floor and he pitched forward almost at the very feet of—of what? An apparition? It could only be the specter of John Henry—once a living man with so much heart and so much brawn he had dared to take on a machine and conquer it. Now, he had returned to the scene of his triumph.

Owens shook with fear, but when he managed to look up, the figure was gone and the tunnel quiet. He was certain he had seen the ghost of John Henry. That night he sought out the old man Banks Terry. He described what had happened and Terry only nodded. Even now, some say that the ghost of John Henry still returns to haunt the Big Bend Tunnel. They say they have heard the sound of his hammers and that his shadowy form stalks along through the darkness, unmindful of the water that slowly drips from overhead to form long and eerie stalactites.

A Visitor from the Dead

Grant Town, West Virginia

Jessie Jackson was a pretty blond girl whose husband was a miner. But John never seemed satisfied to stay at one mine for long. It always looked to him like the grass was greener elsewhere, and that is what sealed his doom.

When John and Jessie came to Grant Town, West Virginia, they moved into one of the mine company houses. It was a monstrous, creaky old place that the company hadn't been able to get anyone else to live in. The last miner who had occupied it years ago died in an accident in the mines and there was talk that the house was haunted. John just laughed at that. He told Jessie they needed all that space for the family they were going to have and he

114

would fix the roof, the sagging front porch, and the rotten floor boards, and the house would be good as new. But Jessie, try as she would, never could seem to make the house look cheerful.

One winter morning Jackson took the lunch his wife had fixed for him and set off for work as usual. It was so cold he could see his breath curl in the air like tobacco smoke. Under his feet the ground was crisp and his boots slid now and then on puddles turned to dirty glass. He had some odd feelings on his way to the mine that morning and he mentioned them to his buddy, Tony Dominec. Although he had just left Jessie, it was like he missed her already. He couldn't understand why he felt so sad.

"You'd think you two was courtin'," joked Tony but he couldn't get a smile out of Jackson, who just shook his head and didn't say a word. They rode the buggy (a small locomotive used to haul coal cars), and when Dominec got off at his level he said, "Meetcha after work." Jackson, who was working one level down, nodded.

It was early afternon when Dominec heard a terrible explosion in the depths of the mine. It seemed to come from beneath his feet and the men near him began running. He ran with them as fast as he could through the tunnel toward the main line. There he saw other miners racing through the main tunnel. Had a fire started on the level below? Would it spread? Would the main tunnel soon be filled with smoke?

Just ahead of him he saw men jumping into the buggy. His chest hurt, his legs felt as if they would give way under him, but he kept running and he managed to get into one of the last cars. When he reached the surface, he began looking for Jackson but he was nowhere to be found. By now wisps of smoke were coming out of the mouth of the mine.

The next morning there were knots of people standing around the entrance to the tunnel—the families of miners who had not come out on the buggy and several of the top men in the coal company. Jessie Jackson was there with her two little boys, waiting to hear whether the rescue crew that had gone into the mine would find any of the missing men still alive. Finally, they came out of the mine. They had found the place were the explosion had occurred, but the men near it had all been burned to death and John Jackson was one of them.

Times were hard and Jessie had only a little money to support herself and the two children. The spring after John's death she married Bill James, who had been one of her husband's close friends. Jessie would get up early, pack Bill's lunch, and off he would go to work at the mines. Then she would go back to bed for a while. About six months after her remarriage, Jessie began to see the ghost of her first husband. Each morning after she went back to bed the ghost would appear in a rocking chair near her. He would sit there staring for a while and then disappear. Jessie was so frightened she couldn't move. This went on for over a month, until she became more and more upset and had to be treated by the mining company doctor.

The doctor thought a change might be good for her and advised her to leave Grant Town for a few weeks and go home to visit her parents. When she returned, she and her husband moved into a new house about half a mile from her old home. Several weeks went by and much to her relief the ghost did not appear. But one morning she had just gone back to bed when she happened to look over at the rocker and there sat the apparition of her dead husband. She screamed and the specter disap-

peared, but the very next morning it was there again.

"What do you want? Tell me!" the terrified Mrs. James cried out.

The ghost motioned with his hand for her to come with him. Upset as she was, she put on her coat quickly and began to follow the shadowy figure down the road. The ghost kept ten or fifteen feet ahead of her, drifting noiselessly but purposefully along, there was no mistaking the fact that the spirit of her first husband seemed to know where it was going. Despite her fear she went on, and when the ghost turned off on the road that led to the mine, she turned, too.

As she arrived, she was just in time to see her second husband standing with a group of other miners waiting to get into the buggy that would take them into the mine. She called him over to her and explained how she had been led here by the ghost. Her husband became angry, for by now he thought all of this was some sort of foolishness. But Jessie began to tremble so, that he decided to take her to the doctor himself.

About lunchtime, when Bill and Jessie returned to the mine, they saw a crowd gathered around the entrance. Some of the women were crying as they held babies in their arms while others had children clinging to their skirts. Right after they had left, ten men had been buried in slate that had fallen from the roof of one of the tunnels, the very tunnel Bill James would have been working in that day. Jessie fell into her husband's arms and began to sob with relief.

If it had not been for the ghost of her first husband, her second would have died along with the other miners. They were both convinced that his ghost had returned from the dead to save Bill James's life, and from then on they placed flowers on his grave regularly.

The Ghosts of Shut-In Creek

Black Mountain, North Carolina

There is a place near Hot Springs in Madison County, North Carolina, that's haunted, "been haunted since I was a boy," said the white-haired old man.

"It may have started right after what happened to my uncle. He worked in a manganese mine up beyond Hot Springs at what they called Dry Branch. One mornin' they let my uncle down in the mine with the wooden box. He'd go down to the bottom, dig out manganese, and load it in the box until it was full and then they'd windlass the box back up.

"When a man would fill the box full, he'd shake the rope, and they kept waitin' and waitin' for my

120

uncle to shake that rope but he never did. They began to holler down into the shaft and it was like a voice would holler up, but it was just their own calls comin' back at them. My uncle never did answer.

"Finally, they put hooks on ropes and let themselves down, and after awhile they managed to bring him up. But he was dead. Nobody knew for sure, but some said gas must have formed down there the night before and that's what killed him.

Shut-In Creek.

"They brought him up to the little old log house on the side of the mountain where he lived and they laid him out, a corpse. There was a real crowd there that night. Some sat inside with the body. Others just stood around the outside the house. I took a turn sittin' inside. Always heard you ought to do that to keep the cats off the corpse, but the lamp in that room kept goin' out even after my aunt brought in a fresh cleaned one. That light goin' out began to work on me some, so I asked her to get someone else to take my chair and set a spell and I went on outdoors.

"We were all standin' around talkin' when someone called out, 'Looky there, comin' right down the mountain!' I looked and saw this big light. Then it started to roll over and over and it was big as a barrel. It was just a-rollin' comin' down toward us. It rolled over and over and over and everybody began to holler. But not my uncle's brother, Ben, and it was comin' at him p'int-blank.

"I don't know whether he'd been drinkin' or what, but he begun to curse that light with it rollin' off the hill toward him. And when he did, well, it hit him, knocked him down, and just kept on rollin' right down the side of the mountain and across the road. Some of them boys standin' nearby lit out runnin' and those of us that stayed 'cause we were too scared to move, we picked Ben up and took him inside. But he never did recover and he died later that night.

"The home place is still there near Shut-In Creek, and it's been haunted ever since. Comin' along that road through there at night certain times of the year, certain nights, you could hear people talkin'. I was comin' through there one night—my, it was dark—and I heard some people talkin' and it sounded like there was a passel of them. It was right near my uncle's house. I kept walkin' expectin' to meet somebody, but I never did meet anybody. I told some folks about that later and a lot of people said, 'Why, I've heard that talkin' many a time.'

"You go about four miles beyond Hot Springs and then you turn to the left. That's Shut-In Creek and the haunted place is down aways about five miles. I wouldn't walk through there again at night, no matter what you gave me. They say the talkin' still goes on near that farm. You hear voices that seem like they move along the road right near you, but you never see a livin' soul."

Highway 19, Where Apparitions Still Ride

Flatwoods, West Virginia

The driver of the truck tried his CB radio again. "Breaker 19, Breaker 19, for north-bounder on Highway 19." Another West Virginia trucker's voice crackled back over the CB radio. "You got a south-bounder. This is the Big Driver." "How's it lookin' over your shoulder, good buddy?" asked Craig Tolliver. "It's clean and green back to Roanoke" came the reply. This was trucker's CB lingo for the fact that there were no patrol cars, accidents, or hazards over the stretch of road Tolliver would soon be traveling.

He had heard some weird stories about this area. His truck tended to hug the inside curve of the mountain road for he knew that a steep drop lay to the left of his cab. A few miles ahead was the hill that had brought death to more than one driver—two of them truckers like himself. It was not the road itself that presented the hazard. It was something far more mystifying.

His big trailer truck began the slow climb up the hill. Why should he be so apprehensive? He had driven this road near Flatwoods, West Virginia, many a time and the trip had always been uneventful. Surely it was only chance that there had been more than one accident along here. The truck went more slowly than usual tonight. Did it too feel reluctant to reach the stretch of highway ahead? What foolishness, he thought. He was overtired, for there was always tension in driving a truck this heavily loaded, and the steel girders he was carrying weighed over twenty-two tons. No wonder the truck was slow to respond on the up grade and tended to hurtle forward as he went down the hills.

Tolliver strained to see ahead. Now he was approaching the crest of the hill. As he reached it, he saw a sight so amazing he could hardly believe his eyes. Halfway down the incline, in his lane, was a wagon pulled by four horses. On the seat was a man and beside him a woman with long hair wearing a white dress. He realized with horror that there was not a way in the world he could avoid hitting that wagon.

He was in low gear, and although he knew it was futile, he pressed the brake as hard as he could. As he went down the grade coming closer and closer to the wagon, his brakes began to burn. Why didn't the wagon turn into the other lane? It contin-

ued its slow and measured pace. He thought of trying to go around it but he knew the weight of the steel girders would send him hurtling over the embankment. He would never be able to pull back in his own lane ahead of it.

He knew in another half minute the couple and their horses would all be one indistinguishable, bloody mass beneath the huge wheels of his truck. Tolliver felt a sudden wave of nausea and as if he were about to black out. In another second he would feel the impact. There was no way to avoid the collision.

Then, much to his astonishment, horses, wagon, and the couple all disappeared at the very moment he was braced for the impact! The moon came out and the road was illuminated behind him. As he looked in his mirror he could see that there was nothing there. What had happened? Where had the wagon and the couple gone? He knew that he had seen them as clearly as he had ever seen anything in his entire life.

It was only a short distance down the road to the truck stop where he had sometimes paused to refuel or for a cup of hot coffee. He needed that coffee tonight as he had never needed it before. When he lifted it steaming hot to his lips, his hands shook so that they spilled the coffee on the counter.

"You seem pretty shaken up, fellow, what's the trouble?" said a voice next to him. He turned to look at the man who had spoken.

"You a trucker?" he asked him. The man said, "No, I'm from over at Flatwoods, a few miles from here. Just thought I'd stop in and grab a sandwich."

Tolliver shook his head as if he would clear his mind.

"You know, if I didn't have good sense, I'd say I been seeing things and ought to be put away."

"What do you mean?"

Had it been another trucker he would have been too embarrassed to talk about it, but what difference did this old man make? He'd go back to the boondocks of Flatwoods, West Virginia, and nobody in his company would ever be any the wiser.

"You won't believe this, but comin' down that road a few miles back I was dead sure I was goin' to run right over the top of a wagon pulled by four horses." The man didn't look surprised.

"Was there a couple on the seat and the girl wearing a white dress?"

"There sure was," said the suprised Tolliver. "How'd you know that?"

"I've heard that story ever since I was a child. I was on that road one night when I was a young man on my way home from calling on my girl. It was bright moonlight and up ahead of me I saw an old wagon moving slowly up the hill. There was a man and a girl in a white dress with long yellow hair hanging to her waist. Their wagon was pulled by four white horses and it was loaded down with heaps of things like pioneers would carry. Those horses were milk white and when they came closer I could see they wore black harnesses with shiny brass studs. It was the strangest sight I ever saw. Just about the time I was close enough to hail them, that wagon disappeared and there was nothing on the road at all. It was a sight I'll never forget if I live to

Truck drivers never know when the phantom will be around the next curve on Highway 19.

be a hundred. Every now and then somebody sees it. My grandfather told me when that road was no more than a trail, a young couple decided to settle up in here and they were on their way to camp for the night near Hacker's Creek when a band of Indians attacked and killed them, leaving their bodies beside the road.

"Every so often, when the moon is bright on certain nights, I've heard tell of that wagon being seen on top of the hill and it has caused some bad accidents there. Sometimes, I wonder about that couple, who they were and why they keep coming back."

The old man shook his head, drained the last drop from his coffee mug, and left.

The Mysterious Face on the Wall

Grant Town, West Virginia

Nick Yelchick would have laughed if you had told him he would ever see a ghost. He was a big, strapping fellow who liked to brag a lot, and if he had too much to drink, it was better to stay away from him. After five years of working for the railroad, in March of 1927 he lost his job and began to find that the bottle helped him forget it. He would stop at a bootleggers in the late afternoon, have a few drinks, and then head home with his own jug.

Whenever he was drunk he would get angry over trifles, beat his wife, and tear up the house. This went on for several months. In the daytime he went out looking for work and finally was able to get one of the West Virginia mines to take him on.

132

The first week everything seemed to go well. The hours were long and the work took plenty of physical strength, but that didn't bother him. He had always made friends quickly, and although the other men would wink at each other when Nick started bragging, most of them liked him. And, at home things were better because he wasn't drinking.

But on Friday at lunch he asked one of his buddies to punch his timecard for him after work that afternoon for he wanted to get to his liquor supplier. His friend promised to do so.

Nick sat down to eat his lunch, and as he was eating one of the sandwiches Anna had packed for him, he began to think of some of the other tunnels where the men had been working that might be easier to mine.

He went down to the level below his own tunnel and inspected the walls as he walked. Other tunnels led off the main one and he turned down one of these, then down another and another before he realized he had lost his way. Aware he was lost, he began to panic and try desperately to get back to the main line. He had walked for several hours when the thought struck him that nobody would be looking for him because he had asked his buddy, John Avangio, to punch his timecard for him. No one would know he was still down in the mine.

After he had walked until what must have been late that night, his light burned out. Now he was in total darkness and he lost his self-control, shouting and shouting until his voice became a whisper. He knew he should wait until morning but he couldn't

stop. Finally, he was so exhausted he was too tired to walk any further. He slumped down against the wall of the tunnel and fell fast asleep.

He was awakened by a strange dream. He had dreamed that he saw his wife's face before him and as he stared into the blackness he saw a luminous spot gradually take shape on the wall of the tunnel and his wife's face stared back at him. He put his arms across his face, convinced that he must still be dreaming, and then he heard her voice and she was saying, "Follow me." Her face began to move along the wall of the tunnel and, frightened though he was, he managed to get up and walk toward it. The eyes shone out at him and the lips seemed to move again forming the words, "Follow me, follow me."

Down one tunnel and then another he went, the face staying just ahead of him. This went on for what must have been over an hour until, at last, he found himself on the main line once more. He looked for the face but it had disappeared. When he arrived at the surface of the mine the night watchman said, "What you been doin' down there, Nick? Your wife was here lookin' for you yesterday, but I seen your card was punched and I told her you had left."

When Nick got home, the first thing he saw was his wife lying across the bed. He went over to wake her, thinking she must have been up all night. When he shook her she didn't move, and then he realized she was dead. On the kitchen table he found a note that said, "Nick, I thought you would stop drinking when you got this job but now I know better."

Nick Yelchick collapsed in a chair, and with his arms on the table he began sobbing, for he knew now that it was his wife's ghost that had come to lead him out of the mine and save his life. From that day on he was a changed man, until he died in Grant Town over twenty years later.

The Specter's Vengeance

Ducktown, Tennessee

A few hours before John Lyons had loaded up the last of his ore at the Copperhill Mine at Ducktown, Tennessee. His blond hair fell over his eyes as he hunched forward, feeling the pull of his team of horses, for the load was a heavy one. He was a good-natured young man and the money he was making hauling ore would soon be enough for a small farm for himself and the girl in Kingsport whom he planned to marry. His mind dwelt happily upon these things.

But the ride to the river was not to be the quiet one he had expected and his musings were soon interrupted by apprehension.

136

Robbers had been waylaying wagons near here and driving the horses and wagons over the cliff after robbing the bodies of the dead drivers. Lyons, like most of the teamsters in eastern Tennessee and North Carolina, was well paid for hauling ore from the mine to the river dock. He patted his money belt uneasily, and as darkness fell across mountains and valleys, every shadow seemed ready to leap out at him.

Thinking he heard sounds other than the creaking of his wagon wheels, he looked around expecting to see robbers at any moment. It was not his imagination, for another wagon was following his. Acting on impulse he decided to pull over into the woods and let it pass. As he waited, he saw it come into view in the moonlight. It was loaded high with copper ore and on the seat sat the figure of a huge man. The fellow wore a dust-covered jacket, secured by one button, and a broad-brimmed, black felt hat.

Lyons stared curiously at the face, and at first glance was appalled by its pallor and staring eyes. But as he watched, the features seemed to spring to life. The mouth broke into a smile and the hollow eyes lit up. The features were strangely familiar. The man obviously meant him no harm and it was good to have company on this road, he thought gratefully.

But not far away from the landing on the river, where the boats were loaded to carry ore to the smelter in Chattanooga, the band of outlaws was already lying in wait. They stood well back in the brush along the banks of the creek where the road

from the mine crossed it. Whispering and grumbling they waited.

"I told you John Lyons would be the last teamster away from Ducktown tonight. Poor fellow, hauling that last lonesome load of copper to the landing," their leader smirked. But his words froze on his lips as he watched the wagon cross the ford. Neither the horse's hoofs nor the wagon wheels splashed the placid surface, but, instead, the wagon appeared to glide over the water.

"Must be turrible low water over that rock," one of the men said. Another spoke up. "Look at that driver, boys. Recognize him, Lem?"

"I think so, but I can't say for sure. He looks strung out, don't he?"

While they watched, a second wagon appeared and took the ford almost in one leap without a call to the horses or a splash. Just as the leader of the robber band raised his pistol, a third wagon appeared. The robbers by now were thoroughly bewildered, for they had expected only John Lyons. Almost as much in fear as to signal the attack, the leader pulled the trigger.

His men swept down, encircling the doomed wagons. In the manner Indians attack, they galloped in a circle around them. Almost in slow motion the three teamsters reached into their wagons and pulled out their rifles, each aiming in a different direction. Before they could fire, the encircling band of outlaws cut loose with their six-shooter revolvers.

The report of gunfire echoed off the mountainside and three of the robbers lay dead from

their own bullets. A moment later the wagons vanished as if they had never been there and the night was quiet. The silence was suddenly broken by the sound of a teamster whip and yet another wagon

rolled along, heading for the ford. The driver drove it with a certain bold abandon and a broad smile upon his face as he headed straight for the landing.

The remaining two outlaws were stunned. Surely, this must be Lyons' wagon and now things would go their way. They began emptying their revolvers at the driver who cracked his whip repeatedly in some sort of wild exultation.

He smiled gleefully as bullets whizzed toward him and his crackling whip gave off tiny sparks in the moonlight. "Keep on firing, boys!" he shouted. His whip touched the tree branches and sent them shivering and rustling. As John Lyons watched from a safe distance back beside the road, he thought he saw the tip of the whip stroke each branch and the leaves sparkle like Fourth of July fireworks. Red and gold bursts of flame, followed by tiny sparks, floated down, struck the rocks in the stream, and faded into extinction. Then all was quiet, for the last of the robbers had fled.

John Lyons was filled with awe. He had recognized some of the drivers of the wagons that passed him, but the reason for his astonishment was that they were all dead! They were the drivers who had been murdered here during the past two years. If it had not been for them, by now he too would probably have been murdered. His life had been saved by a phantom wagon train.

The Angel of Death

Mountains, South Carolina

Patty McCoy was chilled to the bone, but it was not the September night as much as the words she had just heard: "Beware of the cemetery gates, for they will bring death!" She was terrified, for the gates of the cemetery were opposite the McCoy house. The only light in the room came from the kerosene lamp. The witchwoman's skin was seamed and leathery. One eye stared fiercely straight ahead and the other veered off into space with a fiercely malevolent look.

"I see you as a child full of joy," said the woman, "Then as a young girl, when you first met your husband. You wore a blue crocheted shawl the night he asked you to marry him. Isn't that so?" Patty nodded. "He's still a likely-favored man. Is he not?" Patty's eyes filled with tears at the thought of him sitting at sundown on the porch, his banjo in his lap, playing the tunes he loved. He had been ill for almost a year and that was the reason she had come here for advice. Today Bradley was to go to the hospital.

"There is one thing you must never let happen," warned the old woman in her rasping voice, head thrust forward. "I know your homeplace well and the gates of that cemetery are right across the road from it. When they take him to the hospital, don't you let them open that gate. If you do, he's going to die. For what's inside those gates will never rest until it gets him."

Patty put her hand over her mouth to keep from screaming. People had always said, "That Patty, She ain't afeard of nothin'." But now she was afraid. She put a fifty-cent piece in the woman's hand and left.

All she could think about was whether they had come yet to get Bradley. She had been gone for almost two hours. The witchwoman had prepared bits of bone, feathers, roots before she would tell her what to do about Bradley. Patty had no sooner reached the edge of the woods and the open field across which she could see the house when she gave a shriek. For out in front of the porch was a small, dusty ambulance to take him to Louisville. She began to run. Her breath came fast and her heart pounded. She was halfway up the road to the house when the front door opened and two men bearing a stretcher with Bradley carried it down the front steps and placed it in the back of the ambulance.

She screamed out at them, "Wait! Don't take my Bradley 'til I tell ye about the gate." The men looked at her strangely but waited. Now she stood beside them and for a moment was too breathless to warn them about what the witchwoman had told her. She looked at Bradley lying so still on the stretcher, his face the color of putty.

"Kin ye holp him?" asked Patty. The ambulance driver, a tall, red-haired man with watery blue eyes, looked down at her expressionlessly and nodded.

"Well, there ain't no turn-around up here," said Patty. "And when ye git that ambulance down to the road, whatever ye do, don't open the gate of the cemetery to back in. Do ye hear me?"

The driver and his helper got in the ambulance and Patty watched as they backed it down the narrow mountain trail. When they reached the road they must have tried three or four times to back and cut sharp so the ambulance could head out. One of the men finally stood by the side of the road hollering at the other, "If'n you'll just open that gate, we won't have no trouble." But Patty had taken down the shotgun from over the fireplace just as a precaution, run down the road after them, and now stood squarely in front of the gate.

The driver of the ambulance looked at her and at the shotgun, cut the wheels of the ambulance hard, and this time he made it. Patty stood with her back against the cemetery gate and watched the ambulance until it was out of sight. Then she turned and gazed down the road and up the hill toward the cemetery. It was dusk, and as she looked up toward the markers on the crest, she shuddered. What could possibly be up there that could harm

her Bradley? A wind sprang up rustling the tree leaves. It felt chilly for this time of year. Patty shivered and watched the shadows from the cypress trees begin to merge into the coming darkness. Then she turned and walked up the road toward home.

A week later she went to town with Joe Hartley and they brought Bradley back from the hospital in his old pick-up truck. Bradley looked lots better and talked like he felt pretty good, but by the time he was jounced all the way home in the truck, Patty saw he was tired. He wouldn't lie down none though. Said he had to get out and hoe their fall garden. She saw he just needed to do something, so she let him be.

Bradley acted like he was tired a lot of the time and he was a little "tetchy" which wasn't like him. Before he always let her know he was sorry if he saw something he'd said discomfited her, but he didn't talk much now and seldom said anything about the future, like how he was going to buy the land next to theirs and clear it or build another room on to the small cabin nor did he ever hug her about the waist as he used to do and tell her she was still the "likeliest favored gal" he ever saw.

Less than two month later he was down in the bed again, so tired that the littlest thing seemed to make him too weak to lift his head. The doctor wanted him to go to the hospital and Patty wanted to try to get him on the mend at home, but finally she agreed that he should go. She waited with Bradley, holding his hand until the ambulance could get there. It was a large, new ambulance this time, but the tall, white-faced, red-haired man got out with a little, short, chesty fellow who looked well able to handle a stretcher even with a big man on it. Patty pushed back a strand of hair that lay across her husband's forehead and then with a jerky, self-conscious motion bent down and kissed his cheek. The men put the stretcher in the back of the ambulance. Patty felt like she was going to cry, and, turning, she went into the house. She heard the slam of the two doors as the men got in the front and the quiet purr of the motor as the ambulance started backing down the road.

Then, she flung herself across the patchwork quilt on the old walnut bed, but she couldn't cry. Her chest hurt and began to heave. She lay there holding her arms tightly around her and shook, but no tears came.

Suddenly, she recalled the gate and what the witchwoman had told her. She was out the door in an instant and running down the rutted trail that led from the house to the road, when she saw the short, heavy set man jump out of the ambulance and start for the gate. She screamed with all her might, but the wind only blew the words back at her. The gate swung open, the ambulance backed in, and was out and gone. The autumn sunlight struck its massive chrome front and nearly blinded her.

She ran toward the gate, pulled it closed, and then leaned on it, looking toward the hill where the bodies of relatives, friends, and parents were buried, She had not been able to keep the gate closed even after what the witchwoman had told her. Patty leaned against it, feeling as if she was going to faint.

Now the wind sprang up with a vengeance. The leaves that had been green and tender two months before when she had stood at this gate made the harsh, rustling sounds of sandpaper rubbing together, like the eerie rasp of the witchwoman's voice saying over and over, "Don't let them open the cemetery gate! Don't let them open the cemetery gate! Don't let them open it!" The voice within her grew more and more shrill until

she felt that she was floating on a sea of madness. Bradley, Bradley . . . she knew she had failed him.

On top of the hill stood a small knot of people huddled together to escape the biting wind of the winter day. It was the graveyard prayer for Bradley McCoy who had died in the ambulance on the way to the hospital. Patty stood near the grave, head bowed.

She was convinced that something had come out of this cemetery three days before. Some dark, stalking thing that refused to be thwarted and it had claimed Bradley McCoy.